ASTROLOGY FOR DOGS
(AND OWNERS)

ASTROLOGY FOR DOGS (AND OWNERS)

WILLIAM FAIRCHILD

ILLUSTRATED BY LALLA WARD

Elm Tree Books London

For Robin

First published in Great Britain 1980
by Elm Tree Books/Hamish Hamilton Ltd
Garden House 57-59 Long Acre London WC2E 9JZ

Copyright © 1980 by Varangian Productions Ltd
Illustrations copyright © 1980 by Lalla Ward

British Library Cataloguing in Publication Data
Fairchild, William
    Astrology for dogs (and owners).
    1. Astrology and pets
    2. Zodiac
    3. Dogs
    I. Title
    133.5'2   BF1728.3
    ISBN 0-241-10380-0

Typeset by Pioneer
Printed and bound in Great Britain by
Redwood Burn Ltd, Trowbridge and Esher

CONTENTS

The author and publishers apologize in advance to all bitches that for the sake of brevity and to avoid repetition the majority of canine characters discussed in this book are referred to as male.

Acknowledgements

The authors and publishers would like to thank the following for permission to quote extracts:

Constable Publishers: *Prince Rupert of the Rhine* by Patrick Morrah

David and Charles Ltd: *The Story of Battersea Dogs Home* by Gloria Cottesloe

David McKay Co Inc (New York): *White House Pets* by Margaret Truman

William Collins & Sons: *The Judy Story* by E. Varley

Hutchinson Publishing Group Ltd: *Petishism* by Kathleen Szasz

Thames and Hudson Ltd: *Animals and Men* by Kenneth Clark

Macmillan Publishers Ltd: *The Story of the Pekinese* by Rumer Godden

FOREWORD

I love this book. It's a must for anyone who has a dog, has ever thought of having a dog, or knows someone who has a dog. It's fun but full of good advice. It's amusing and entertaining but it'll help you (whatever your birth sign) towards a richer relationship with your dog (whatever his). And vice versa. Of course dogs have horoscopes, just the same way that people do, and any other animal for that matter. And like their human counterparts they go through all the ups and downs of life, the frustrations and the joys of courtship, romance, love and sex, the fulfilment of attaining their goals, whether winning a blue ribbon at a local pet show or searching for and finding some long lost treasure (most likely an old bone or shoe); and when troubles occur, waiting in anticipation for that magical moment when all their woes turn to delights and their sorrows to happiness.

Only a Gemini (William Fairchild was born on 1 June) would suddenly decide to switch from writing plays and films to a book about the birth signs of dogs. But as Geminis are always playing at Red Cross, coming to the rescue of friends and strangers alike, I would not be surprised if this one were to receive a citation from the RSPCA for his valuable contribution to more understanding between man and his faithful friend.

As in any relationship, the more you can get to know about your loved ones the better. Naturally there are traits that we are attracted to and find lovable, amusing and intriguing, likewise there are other traits which we wish they would change, that drive us up the wall, make us nervous wrecks and generally spoil our disposition and give us indigestion. Dogs, at times, and depending on their Zodiac sign will have the same effect on us. This book will help you and your dog live together in harmony,

7

understanding and with an idealistic view to the future. Not only should every member of the family read it so that they will forgive the weaknesses and praise the talents of our canine friend, but a daily reading aloud to the dog itself will help him change some of his negative habits and turn them into more positive rewarding ones.

My Prediction? It will be a best seller!

Fredrick Davies.

ꟼNTRODUCTION

I once witnessed a dog saving the lives of twelve men. He was not a St Bernard and was far from any snow. He was in the middle of a dense fog way out in the North Sea, a small white fluffy animal known as a Maltese, a breed which has existed for 3,000 years, possessed of great charm, natural fidelity and a shrill bark. His particular shrill bark guided my destroyer through otherwise impenetrable grey mists to the lifeboat he shared with the entire crew of a Norwegian freighter which had just been sunk by a stray mine. After we'd picked them up the men drank rum and the dog, his coat matted and blackened by oil fuel, peed with ceremony and precision down our hawsepipe, thus proving that he was well ship-trained. His owner, the Norwegian skipper, explained that his whole life had been spent aboard the freighter. What would happen to him now that it was no more? Six months in British quarantine? (With enemy hordes poised to invade the United Kingdom, presumably accompanied by their various dogs, this rule still persisted, a comforting sign of orderliness in a disordered world.) Naturally we agreed to adopt him. 'He is a very little dog,' the Norwegian said in sad farewell, 'but he has the heart of a lion'. He had indeed. That was his LEO influence. But I believe our Maltese had been born around the 23rd or 24th of July, on the cusp of CANCER and LEO, and thus possessed the characteristics of both these signs. (See pages 30 and 32.)

These were, admittedly, an unusual set of reasons for becoming a dog owner. On the whole people tend to have more orthodox ones, some perhaps more logical than others:

To hunt other animals or retrieve those they have just shot.

9

To guard the home.
To encourage physical exercise.

To breed yet more dogs thus making money or winning trophies.
To amuse small children or replace larger ones who have grown
up and moved elsewhere.

To entertain other dogs or replace those who have lived their
day.
To indulge latent power complexes by training them to perform
acts which they are perfectly capable of performing themselves

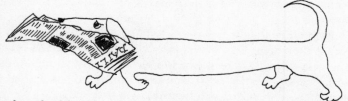

such as fetching the morning newspaper/greeting the postman/
sitting up/lying down/begging for food/pretending to be dead
at the sound of a whistle or word of command.

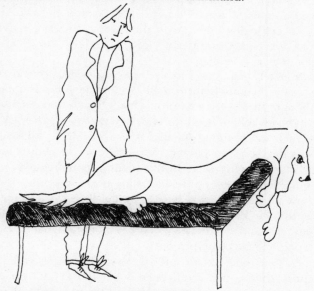

Because their psychiatrist has advised it.
Because they've been given one and feel guilty about trying to
get rid of it.

Because it provides the easiest means of bestowing/receiving love.

Because they're lonely.

Because their lives are overcrowded and they crave one other being who will always be pleased to see them even though their wife/husband/lover/friends/relations/offspring/clients may not. Some, because their dog will furnish them with eyes.

All these reasons have one element in common. The necessity of creating, to a greater or lesser degree, companionship, understanding, a partnership. It's not unlike getting married for a limited number of years. Perhaps, on reflection, not so limited. Today's average dog lives longer than today's average marriage and that, for a start, could say something about the difference between dogs and people.

Basically, a human partnership breaks up because one or both of the partners comes to the conclusion that the other is not what they thought they were when it began. They mutter something about irretrievable breakdown and, hey presto, it's over. A dog has no such soft options. For him it really is till death (usually his own) do part. He has no more freedom of choice in the middle of a tottering relationship than at its optimistic outset, and he had none then. All he has is his awareness of his inmost self, those mysteries he was born with, his character, his nature, his identity. He knows he can never entirely suppress them and although, *pro bono publico*, he will try to moderate them, he can't do it alone. He needs help. Yours.

But do you even consider those mysteries, those vital natal influences when you're acquiring a dog? No way. All you do is pick a certain breed and hope for the best and that's about as crazy as setting up house with an American, a Spaniard or a Russian simply because you're partial to the USA, Spain or the USSR. There are as many different sorts of dogs and bitches in any one breed as there are different sorts of men and women in any one race. Just as Americans can be introverts, Spaniards speculative and Russians reactionary so can there be lazy Labradors, serious-minded Sealyhams, self-conscious Scotties, forgetful Field Spaniels, oversexed Otterhounds, dilatory Dobermanns, neurotic Newfoundlands, amorous Alsatians and yapless Yorkies. You might even come across a Basenji who barks, a communist-orientated Corgi or a Tibetan Terrier that's taciturn. None of these characteristics can be said to have much to do with the breed. They derive from the fact that the Sun was in a particular zone of the Zodiac when the dog in question was born. The influence of their Sun Sign in fact. Of course if you want to get your dog's horoscope *absolutely* right you should also take into account the aspects of the moon and planets, the sign that's rising on the eastern horizon and the position of the twelve Houses at the *precise moment he took his first breath.* (Even puppies of the same litter possess differing natal influences as none are born at *exactly* the same time.) However, since the average breeder is far too busy to keep consulting a stop watch during such activities, you will certainly find all this difficult to verify. Even if you could, you'd then have to give the information to someone capable of constructing your dog's Personal Natal Chart i.e. a professional Astrologer. He'd do it too, with total accuracy and no wisecracks. But good astrologers are pretty busy with humans, and being one yourself, you'd probably rather spend the cash on your own chart first. So, as far as your dog is concerned, why not rely on his Sun Sign for a start anyway?

They are by far the strongest and most influential of the lot and will provide you with at least 80% of that hitherto hidden and priceless knowledge you'll need in order to make a decision which can affect the intrinsic fabric of both your lives.

Suppose, for example, you've made the wrong one. Suppose right now you are the owner of a dog who can't help being attracted by danger, the heady risk of plunging into arguments with other dogs, particularly, being a bit of a show-off, those that are bigger than himself, the Goliaths he encounters in the park. He can't explain this tendency. It's as much a part of his basic nature as his need for food and exercise. But whenever he indulges it, the effect on you, normally an individual of equable temperament, is little short of catastrophic. You lose all self control, start bellowing and cursing, and like an infuriated bull, wade into a battle which had nothing to do with you in the first place. In the process one of your hands will probably be bitten by Goliath and you'll immediately use the other to chastise your own dog. This action will appear to him as supremely illogical and furthermore he will feel deprived of a good clean fight as

well as being humiliated in the face of the enemy. Naturally he will relapse into a fit of the sulks and stubbornly refuse to risk participating in the next walk to the park or anywhere else, preferring to remain in solitude with his own dark thoughts. Equally naturally this attitude adds fuel to the fires of your anger. You may love him but by God he's got to learn that there's an end even to your considerable patience. I'm steadfast you think, nursing your wounded hand, I'm loyal, and if we're going to have anything like a workable relationship he'd damn well better start appreciating it instead of behaving like an exhibitionist dog David every time we set foot outside the door. You may even say all this out loud which will only increase your fury because the wretched animal just sits there and refuses to understand. An unhappy situation, fraught with stress and anguish on both sides. I can't help my nature, your dog thinks, nursing his wounded pride, why can't this man (or this woman) who's picked on me to share their life understand that? They're so damn clever about everything else why weren't they bright enough at the beginning of it all to realize what sort of character I am? He crouches in a corner refusing to budge and your frustration transforms your reasoned requests to get off his butt and come for a walk into harsh hysterical orders and he'll growl or bark or even do something unpleasant on the floor to mark *his* frustration and the odds are you'll rub his nose in it and tell him he's been guilty of a disgusting act. He'll get your exact meaning from the tone of your voice and in view of what's just happened to his face will have good reason for feeling that the boot is surely on the other foot and that two blacks certainly do not make a single white. Mutual resentment grows, Pelion is piled on Ossa, matters already bad become even worse. You wonder how such an endearingly gentle puppy could have turned into this stubbornly pugnacious monster and he vows to tear the next Goliath limb from limb and to hell with the consequences. Impotent sadness envelops you both and you reflect that perhaps after all you are simply not suited to one another and that somewhere along the line there has been a disastrous mistake.

There was, and since dogs can't read you were responsible for making it. But it need never have happened. If you'd taken the trouble to consider your respective Sun Signs you'd have found that yours was Taurus and his was Aries. Such awareness would not have prevented you from buying him, nor should it have done. Many born when the sun is in the sign of the Bull make perfectly happy lives with those born when it is in that of the Ram, whether both are human or one happens to be a dog. What it would have done was provide you with sufficient knowledge, insight and understanding of both your characters and their likely inter-reactions to enable you to guide them painlessly towards their more positive and fruitful potentials whilst avoiding the friction occasioned by their more negative and troublesome ones. In other words, in this instance, to effect a blessed deliverance from battles in the park, bitten hands, hurt pride and the bitter fruits of general misunderstanding.

What is true of the relationship between Taurus and Aries is equally true for that of any of the twelve signs. But remember that natal influences, invaluable though they are as advance information, are no more than that. What you do with it is up to you and your dog. The Signs of the Zodiac, as serious astrologers are always anxious to stress, IMPEL and do not COMPEL. Your dog, his mind uncluttered by man-made theories and higher educational impedimenta, knows the truth of this maxim by instinct. The least you can do is to help him — and yourself — by allowing these ancient inevitable differing causalities to *impel* you both in the right direction.

ARIES

(22nd March — 20th April)

WE'VE already met him, the dog David, the Ram charging into fights with all comers, and been less than fair in first drawing attention to two of his least endearing characteristics, those of pugnacity and sulkiness. But even they spring from far more admirable qualities — directness, complete lack of subtlety, a sort of shining innocence. Put these together with the fact that he's headstrong and brave and you get the fights. Put them with frustration or imagined humiliation and you get stubbornness, the sulks. Other dogs would find ways of avoiding the confrontation we've mentioned. They'd get round you and we all know the methods — an apologetically winsome wiggle of

16

the whole body, the tentative waggle of a droopy tail, a melting look in eyes hitherto downcast as they flicker upwards brimming with unshed tears, heartfelt penitence. Not so with your Aries. He is incapable of dissembling, there is no deviousness in him; he is appalled by injustice and will contest it to the end rather than submit to it. Such dogs may not be the easiest to live with but, on the other hand, they are always stimulating, constantly unpredictable and never boring. In many ways they are also contradictory. Basically egocentric they genuinely enjoy making others happy. Naturally energetic and inventive they lose interest in a new project or idea once they have become accustomed to it. Such conflicting characteristics can lead them into typically awkward Arien situations. Take for instance the classic scene of a contented family throwing a tennis ball to each other on the beach. All are smiling and relaxed, even Dad. Then suddenly their magic circle is invaded by a strange dog who catches the ball in his mouth and rushes off with it, spraying sand into the picnic basket and skittling a small daughter en route. Mum screams that the sandwiches are ruined, daughter bursts into tears, Dad gives chase, falls over his feet and sprains his ankle. The dog, delighted with all the extra activity he has engendered, brings the ball back and deposits it in front of small son, the only member of the family group who has not yet started yelling. Small son refuses to pick it up for fear of getting bitten and the dog prompts him to join in the general jollity by jumping up at him and barking enthusiastically. This totally unnerves the child who immediately sets up a mournful caterwauling louder even than that of his sister. In less than half a minute contentment has become consternation, a smiling, united family reduced to a tearful, divided one. And all because a well-meaning Arien dog wanted to liven up their game and make them even more deliriously happy than they were when he first decided to entertain them. He never intended to make a permanent intrusion on their privacy and if only they'd had the decency to play the game his way for a little while instead of behaving like a crowd of demented banshees, he'd have got bored with them and gone off to improve the lot of someone else. This admirable concern for others can also strike nearer home. Suppose your dog hears an unexpected noise at two o'clock in the morning

(Ariens are alert, intuitive, perceptive). His first thought will be for your safety. If a warning salvo of barks produces no reaction he will run to your room, leap onto the bed and start licking your face. The extent of gratitude he receives for this selfless act will of course depend upon the origin of the noise. A nocturnal prowler attempting to break open the kitchen window with a jemmy is one thing, a lamp on your night table which you've knocked over whilst groping for a second sleeping pill is quite another. In the latter case remember he's an Arien and control your temper.

Prone to cuts

ARIES dogs usually make difficult patients. This is because they so detest the idea of being ill that they refuse to admit it when they are. Give up all thoughts of secreting therapeutic pills in some delicious piece of food. He'll spot such devious ploys straight away and leave the pill on the floor as a warning not to try it again while he gobbles up the rest.

They don't like vets either and, if literally driven to consult one, will put on a convincing show of good health until they're allowed home again. Besides proving expensive this habit will eventually mean that you've run out of friendly neighbourhood vets. But don't despair. If you take a bit of trouble to explain things to him logically (preferably at an early age), you'll find that his good qualities easily outweigh his bad. Ariens can make excellent watchdogs and might even enjoy being shown (that's the actor in them). Their loyalty is unquestionable and if they're well balanced and have come to terms with their own nature they can be reliable Guide Dogs for the blind. It is an Arien characteristic to wish to lead others out of darkness.

Finally, if the going gets tough for you, he'll be right there beside you, offering his support. That's one thing you *don't* have to explain to him. He understands instinctively because a lot of the time it's pretty tough for him too.

DO:
Be patient and explain that it's a dog's life while he's still a puppy.
Keep him on a leash whilst walking on the beach.
Keep your bedroom door shut.
Pretend a visit to the vet is your annual call on the in-laws.

DON'T:
Lose your temper.
Get into *his* fights.
Sulk when he sulks.
Try to deceive him (except about vets).

MOST COMPATIBLE HUMAN SIGNS:
Sagittarius, Leo, Aquarius, Libra.

HEALTH:
(Note: Your dog may well go through life without suffering from *any* of the weaknesses or afflictions mentioned under his sign — but forewarned is forearmed.
If any *should* occur those marked with two asterisks are the most likely. Those marked with one are possible but less likely.)

** Cuts. Kidney infections.
 * Teeth. Eyes. Dietary difficulties.

ᏩᎯᎤᎡᎤᏚ

(21st April — 21st May)

CAUTIOUS, practical, reliable, patient, responsible and determined. These are the key words relating to the character of the average Taurean dog and if you were immediately to assume from them that he would be good for tending sheep, guarding your property, or even, like an Aries, leading the blind, no one could blame you. But pause for a moment's thought before rushing out to buy him. Do you have a garden where midges and other insects congregate during the summer? Do you by any chance keep bees? Is your barn occupied by mice? Are there snails amongst the flowers, slugs around the vegetables? Are you one of those nice people who pick up ladybirds and show them to all and sundry as tokens of good luck? If so don't include your stout-hearted Taurus dog in the audience. He will probably back away with his tail between his legs whimpering like a frightened baby. It's a fact that whilst a Taurus dog is unafraid of any large animal he's absolutely petrified of small ones. I once knew a Pekingese who was born on the first of May. He was an even-tempered little chap but if another dog did something which really angered him like stealing his bone or eating out of his bowl he would go berserk, hurling himself at the intruder's throat regardless of whether he happened to be of the same fighting weight or a well-muscled Great Dane. His behaviour on these occasions was both ridiculous and impressive, literally like that of a bull in a china shop. He didn't know the meaning of the word fear until we were out walking one day and he met an extremely small frog sitting beside a pond. He stopped dead in his tracks. The frog hopped in his direction. The Peke turned and ran, his usually proud tail brushing the ground behind him like a flag of surrender. The next day, on the principle that if one falls off a horse one should immediately remount and try again, I took him for the same walk but when we neared the pond he sat down and refused to budge. I made the mistake of laughing at his fears and he promptly scuttled off home in high dudgeon.

¶T took me the rest of the day to find him. He had got up into the attic and was sitting there with an ancient bone, an old squeaky toy and one half of a rubber ball with which he had played as a puppy. They were spread out in a half circle in front of him like some magic protection against the threat of further devilish frogs. Fortunately I was able to persuade him to come down before he noticed a spider busily weaving a web in the corner behind him.

Apart from this illogical attitude towards small and creeping things, Taurean dogs are great lovers of nature. They are also great lovers of comfort and good red meat so don't try fobbing them off with a bit of linoleum under the kitchen sink or one of the less imaginative tins of something or other. They're not exactly quick witted but when they learn something they do it thoroughly and don't forget it. They have a great need to feel secure in their relationships and if they don't are inclined to compensate by becoming acquisitive and over-possessive, and in extreme cases can display violent jealousy. But if you understand and respond to their basically warm and affectionate natures they will reciprocate and you'll get along fine together. Some Taurean dogs are so predictable that they can become boring and almost all are obstinate, but if you're clever you can use one of these defects to cancel out the other. For instance they insist, like bulls, on conserving their energy whilst you, on the other hand, may wish to tire them out in the hope that they'll sleep at night instead of prowling and sniffing about all over the house like some over-conscientious and asthmatic sentry. There are at least two methods for overcoming their obstinacy in this respect.

Do sell the children's hamsters

The first is to pretend to bury a juicy bone in the garden whilst actually concealing it in your pocket. Your dog will dig for hours before finally collapsing in exhaustion. This ruse however, besides not bearing repetition, tends to ruin the flower beds not to mention your clothes. A better one is to look out of a window and shout the name of your dog's enemy number one. He will almost tear the front door down in order to get at him. If repeated gallops round the empty garden in search of his prey don't quite do the trick you can repeat the deception, this time looking up the stairs. There is only one safety precaution which must be observed. Make sure that enemy number one is not by mischance actually present or you may spend an uncomfortable hour or so trying to separate them. With either ploy of course the moment will arrive when he realizes he's being conned and then you'll have to think of something new. *Never* try the patience of a Taurus dog too far.

DO:
Sell the children's hamsters.
Give him a feeling of security.
Feed him plenty of good red meat.
Draw up subtle plans for overcoming his natural obstinacy.

DON'T:
Own a china shop.
Allow him to become a bore.
Exhaust his patience.
Expect him to come to your rescue when you're standing on a chair because you've seen a mouse.

MOST COMPATIBLE HUMAN SIGNS:
Capricorn, Virgo, Cancer, Scorpio.

HEALTH:
** Colds. Sore Throats.
 * Overeating. Ear-ache.

GEMINI

(22nd May — 22nd June)

CERBERUS was probably a 50% overgrown Gemini. All dogs born under the sign of the Twins start life, if not with multiple heads, certainly with two personalities, two separate identities — and then proceed to live it in two minds trying to do two things at once. With all this duplication of effort it is not altogether surprising that they never succeed in really growing up but retain their puppy charm and puppy limitations well into the senior citizen years. Happily the limitations do not include matters of house training and general hygiene. A Gemini dog will learn where and where not to relieve himself as quickly as any other but take care never to offer him a *choice* of legitimate loos. Such an option will be for him literally an embarrassment of riches and he will keep on darting from one to the other, trying vainly to decide which is the best, until he ends up by either giving himself a stricture or peeing at some totally unsuitable point midway between them. Their charm of course, is devastating and, since your Geminian is well aware of it, he can and will use it for a large variety of purposes ranging from persuading you to dress up like an Arctic explorer in order to take him for a walk in the winter rain (and then changing his mind at the very last moment so that you have to take it all off again) to convincing you that he really can't exist for another day without enjoying the pleasures of sex. Assuming that he succeeds in this latter endeavour (nine times out of ten he will) you, as his proud owner will naturally arrange, for a suitable settlement, that the best-bred bitch in the district shall provide his connubial bliss. Be prepared to return the money. The odds are that he'll leave her standing at the door of the kennel and rush off to enjoy himself with some disreputable lady mongrel, who, whilst distressingly low on social standing, is presumably obligingly high on sexual attractions. It is a sad but undeniable fact that many apparently fatherless puppies were in reality

24

sired by randy but inconstant Gemini dads. Even leaving such questionable activities aside it is true to say that Gemini dogs do need a lot of rest. The sheer ingemination involved in everything they do will tend to tire them out and when at last they go to sleep you may well hear them making strange squeaking noises. Do not be alarmed. This is simply caused by one of their two persona actively dreaming and thus disturbing the other who isn't. Duality is their keynote, variety their necessity. They loathe the drudgery of routine, crave constant change and excitement. Inactivity leads to boredom and boredom results in emotional upsets. You'll always know when one of these is taking place because no Geminian dog will suffer in silence. Everyone must share in and sympathize with his travail until he's decided he's better. But if he's off his food don't give him pills. Try entertaining him with a few jokes instead and if this doesn't get results go for something a bit more drastic like changing the loose covers in the drawing room or repainting the back door.

ELIGHTED by such exciting changes he will snap out of his depression, gobble up everything on his plate and insist on sharing his new found enjoyment of life with you just as he insisted on sharing his previous despair. Geminis feel a tremendous need for communication and like the children they nearly are, keep on asking 'why?'. If you're wise you'll give them an answer, preferably two. It doesn't have to be the literal truth so use your imagination. They adore fantasy anyway. Although they really do want to keep everyone around them happy their friendships with other dogs tend to be superficial. Depending on which of their two personalities is uppermost it's all 'share my bone' one day and 'I don't remember meeting you' the next. This can be particularly awkward if one of the other dog's owners happens to be someone of importance to you. More than one human relationship has foundered on the rocks of canine incompatability. Occasionally they will even behave in the same way towards you, changing without warning from warm affection to cold stand-offishness. But this is only a trick, a means of creating a bit of variety in order to satisfy curiosity, and it won't last. Memories are not their strongest point. If you mate a Gemini bitch and she enjoys it (odds on she will) mate her again as soon as practicable before she's forgotten the essential details of what it's all about and driven herself distracted with frustration. In the meanwhile rest assured that she will look after her puppies with real motherly affection — providing you're there to remind her where they are. A few Geminian dogs are capable of developing such split personalities that half the time they think they are cats. This can lead to unfortunate misunderstandings if you happen to own a cat as well. But in spite of all their Mercurial qualities you can absolutely rely on one thing — no Gemini will ever bore you and if you can put up with a lot of furious activity for its own sake and cope with quicksilver changes of mood for no immediately apparent reason you should be very happy together — providing, of course, that you never bore him. A final piece of advice. Don't ever let him feel left out. Talk to him. Make him feel he's wanted. He'll really appreciate that — and he'll let you know it.

DO:
Explain what you want (truthfully) and why (entertainingly).
Try and take him away at weekends.
Give him plenty of exercise. (No need for you to exert yourself. He'll make all the running — either round you in circles or racing with his other half.)
Take him in the car (window low enough to permit inquisitive examination of the passing show but high enough to prohibit premature leap into it).
Understand that you've got two dogs for the price of one.

DON'T:
Live in a small high rise flat.
Leave him alone all day while you're working nine to six.
Waste your money on an expensive basket or a smart kennel — they'll just make him feel trapped.
Wake him up at night because you thought you heard a burglar.
Expect him to hear the burglar first.

MOST COMPATIBLE HUMAN SIGNS:
Aquarius, Libra, Sagittarius.

HEALTH:
** Insomnia. Nervous Exhaustion.
 * Lung troubles.

CANCER

(23rd June — 23rd July)

WHETHER you're in the serious breeding business or just want to get your hands on some puppies to amuse the kids/give to people who already have everything else/sell in order to balance the dog food budget, you'd be well advised to start with a bitch who's birthday falls between 23rd June and 23rd July when the sun is in the sign of the Crab. They're natural mothers and they'll guard, protect and pamper their offspring in a fashion which would put most humans to shame (unless they're Cancer Mums too). But do *not* allow your young to treat theirs as playthings. Mother might not appreciate it. And for Heaven's sake be careful when the moment comes to take their babies away from them. Do it tactfully, gently, and with much prior reassurance and patient explanation. Not that your bitch will bite you. Nothing as simple and direct as that. She'll feel deeply hurt, retreat into her Crablike shell and mope. Whereas bites can be cured in a matter of days, a full-blooded Cancerian mope can last for weeks or even months. Cancer dogs may look tough but that's just the shell again. Underneath they're moody, insecure, sensitive and compulsive worriers. You may notice one mooning about the place with drooping tail, tracing and retracing his steps while his face assumes an increasingly grave and concerned expression. Don't imagine that he's sickening for some dread disease. He's simply feeling guilty because he can't find anything to worry about and is desperately trying to think of something. Apart from this, Cancerian dogs don't really think very much. They're far too busy feeling or remembering. The security of family life (yours as well as theirs) is immensely important to them and once they feel they're part of it you'll enjoy their affection for ever. They'll grow to love your home too but, by itself, this is not enough. They'll require their own personal domain within it and if you're wise you'll provide them with a kennel or basket depending on their size. Don't waste money furnishing them. An old cushion or two is all that's necessary and they'll do the rest, filling their pad with their own treasured possessions and mementoes. And whatever you do, don't rush to the pet shop and buy one of those new-fangled toys because you think they'll enjoy playing with it. They won't. They don't like new things, only old ones, the older the better. It might be a chewed up slipper or a gnawed and ancient bone and however unsavoury or insanitary such objects may appear, you'll have to learn to live with them because for him they are his prized lares and penates, the ultimate in Dog Home Furnishings. You'll get a king size Mope if you try to throw them away, and you'll deserve it. They represent a part of his security. Another part is food. Always take care not to run out. If supplies are getting short he will sense it (he's psychic) and start storing whatever scraps he can find in secret and inconvenient places against future emergencies.

EVEN when stocks are high he'll never waste anything and is well known for trying to lick the pattern off his bowl after the end of a meal. If you leave your own plate with a bit of meat or some vegetables still on it and he starts asking for it, don't tick him off for being greedy. It's just that he cannot

bear to see any food thrown away. Give it to him and he'll clean
it up even at the risk of severe indigestion.

They'll love and play with your children almost as much as
with their own. Watch them on the beach together. That dog will
swim out to sea after sticks till the kids are too exhausted to keep
on throwing them. But he won't be *entirely* happy unless you're
there too, lying on your mattress and soaking up the sun. It's no

Don't leave him in a thunderstorm

good being irritated when he dashes out of the surf and shakes
himself all over you and your new paperback. He only does it in
order to make sure that you're still there, that the *whole* family is
still present. Later, when you've at last managed to drop off to
sleep he may well come and bark in your ear. Take a look
around before you wallop him. He can remember smells and
events like he can remember feelings, and the chances are that
he's warning you to get moving before the tide comes right in
and cuts you off. If you have a boat and he refuses to get aboard,
take a look at the weather forecast or the sky. It'll be odds on that
the clouds are darkening and the wind's getting up. Cancer dogs
feel such things, particularly when they have to do with the sea.
Like that Maltese we picked up from his lifeboat. Although he
seemed to have settled for a new life in our ship he spent most of
the one day we had in port during our short time together
running down to the jetty or jumping onto the Motor Torpedo
Boat which was moored on the other side. He never tried to go
any further but just stood looking up at us on our deck as though
hoping we'd join him. At the time we thought he must be
searching for his old master but it wasn't that. I am sure he had

somehow guessed what was going to happen and wanted to warn us. Anyway two nights later my ship was sunk by a bomb, rather ignominiously in the middle of Portsmouth harbour. By a miracle no one was hurt and the dog sat in the bows of the large boat which finally took us ashore. There was no trace of 'I-told-you-so' in his expression. That belonged to the Cancer side of his nature. Now, faced with a totally different sort of situation, he was suddenly all Leo.

DO:

Allow him to keep his favourite toy/bone/slipper no matter how disgusting it may look.

Take him for a day by the sea whenever you can. Better, buy a cottage on the coast. Better still, a boat. Best of all — both.

Let him guard the children.

Listen to his 'voices'.

DON'T:

Go out and leave him alone when there's thunder in the air.

Acquire a Cancerian dog if you're about to get divorced or your children are thinking of leaving home.

Be fooled by that seemingly tough protective shell.

Live in the geographical centre of Britain or worse still in that of America.

MOST COMPATIBLE HUMAN SIGNS:
Scorpio, Pisces, Taurus, Capricorn.

HEALTH:
** Imaginary illnesses.
 * Chest complaints. Stomach ulcers.

♌ LEO

(24th July — 23rd August)

HE looked like a small, proud white figurehead and when we reached the jetty he was the first to jump ashore, showing the rest of us the way, a natural leader. There was another air raid that night and we were required to obey regulations by going down into a deep shelter. We were unaccustomed to this and so was the dog. But if he felt uneasy (as I did) he didn't show it. Instead, he decided to put on a performance of tremendous vitality, rushing round the cavernous cellar, wagging his tail like mad, licking peoples hands when they greeted him, barking at them when they didn't. 'Gutsy little character,' said a very senior Naval officer, 'sets a

damn good example. Where's he sprung from?' No one volunteered the information that he was the survivor of two sunken ships. Sailors, even those of high rank, are inclined to be superstitious and in any case we had our own plans for him. One of my CPO's who had two elderly maiden aunts living alone in a remote part of the country, had assured me that they would welcome the gift of a good guard dog. I asked no questions and the word 'quarantine' was never mentioned but I feel sure that the old ladies slept easier with that gutsy little character to look after them and perhaps they even managed to take him down to the sea for a paddle sometimes.

L EOS *are* good guard dogs. They don't go out looking for fights like Ariens, but remain in situ waiting for trouble to come to them and in this respect they take their responsibilities as seriously and wholeheartedly as in any other. When they're guarding, they *guard*, when they're playing they *play*, when they're resting they *rest*, when they're entertaining they do it in the grand manner — and woe betide anyone who falls short of their regal standards. I once attended a dinner party given by an elderly couple who owned a Leo dog of normally irreproachable social behaviour. They had no domestic help, did the cooking themselves and the guests helped with the washing up, but it was a long established rule of the house that everyone *dressed.* Black ties for the men, long dresses for the women. On this occasion one unfortunate lady arrived in a short one. The dog was scandalized and, to make quite sure that she would never repeat the error if asked again, kept reminding her of it by sniffing up her abbreviated skirts at every possible opportunity. She *was* asked again but pleaded a previous engagement. Leo dogs like an ordered existence, preferably having given the orders themselves. This attitude can get out of hand if not understood and corrected early on. It's great to be loved by a Leo dog but do take care that his possessiveness doesn't smother you. His basic need to run things his way can mar even an affectionate relationship. He can't help feeling superior. It's his nature. But someone has to be the boss so make sure it's you, otherwise you might as well buy yourself a collar and leash and

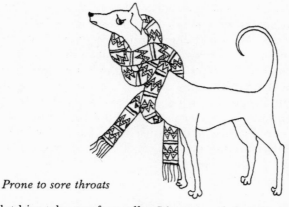

Prone to sore throats

let him take *you* for walks. It's no good shouting orders at him. Leo dogs are far too proud simply to obey commands because they're loud. In order to make him do what you want you must find his Achilles heel — his vanity — and work on it. Flattery will get you everywhere and it can take several forms. Try racing him across a field and then arrange to fall when you're half way (you might as well because unless you're Olympic class he'll beat you anyway). He'll come tearing back and stare at you in an infuriatingly smug and patronizing manner. Keep your temper and tell him he's got to be the fastest thing on four legs since Mick the Miller. He'll feel so pleased with himself that he'll do anything you ask for the next half hour at least. Alternatively you could give him a really comfortable bed or an absolutely splendid feeding bowl. Leo dogs adore and respond to luxury. If they could book airline tickets they'd never choose Economy. A third method is to stand him in front of a mirror whilst you're brushing him and make ooh and aah noises of enthusiastic admiration. You'll have him eating out of your hand. Incidentally there's a lot of the ham actor in them and they make excellent show dogs. But they like to be the Star so if they don't win a first prize pretty quickly, stop pushing them. They'll feel insulted and take it out on you later. They're brave and romantic and larger than life and their hearts are the hearts of lions. If you can accept them on these terms whilst refusing to allow them to dictate theirs, you'll walk and run and laugh with kings.

DO:

Remember that he has a superiority complex.

Show him if you wish — but be prepared to bribe the judges if you're doubtful about his chances.

Love him with sincerity.

Flatter him with guile.

DON'T:

Get a Leo dog if you already have an inferiority complex.

Remove a bone that he's hidden.

Laugh at him.

Shout like a Sergeant Major.

MOST COMPATIBLE HUMAN SIGNS:

Aries, Sagittarius, Aquarius.

HEALTH:

** Spinal weakness. Back troubles.

 * Sore throats.

Don't remove a bone that he's hidden

VIRGO

(24th August — 23rd September)

BEFORE deciding to buy a Virgo dog it is as well to face the fact that he will be *fussy* about practically everything from his personal cleanliness to that of his food, from his work (if he does any) to his choice of a mate (if he consents to make one). This meticulousness, this minute attention to detail, if not checked or redirected at an early stage, can develop to the point of downright irritation. The best idea is to encourage him to channel it into some sort of useful activity. Virgos are very hard workers and could, for example, become excellent sheepdogs, particularly as they never seek the limelight but actually enjoy labouring in the background. They don't show people (or sheep) the way but they do make absolutely sure that they don't stray far from it. If one of their charges gets out of line by even a yard they'll have him right back in place before you can say 'three bags full'. This may annoy the more cavalier sheep but it will certainly satisfy the shepherd. Obviously not all Virgoans can be sheepdogs but do try to find something over which they can fuss thus preventing them from fussing unduly over you (which *might* ruin your relationship) or, worse still, fussing in general because they can't think what to fuss about in particular (which *definitely* will).

AS far as food is concerned they are a mixture of Taurus and Cancer. It must be wholesome and well served and *never* on any account be wasted. You cannot fool a Virgo dog by wrapping up still edible scraps in a plastic bag and flinging the whole lot with casual confidence into the dustbin. He'll simply wait till you've left the room, upset the bin, open the bag and remove the contents to his bowl where he'll arrange them neatly before starting to eat. And don't make the further mistake of adding insult to injury by blaming him for the mess on the

36

kitchen floor. It's your fault for committing the sin of unnecessary waste in the first place and if you try to shift the responsibility onto him he'll just remove himself from your presence until you've apologized. Any Virgoan would rather be alone than with someone they find objectionable. This is a part of their chaste reclusive side and is most clearly evidenced in matters of sexual behaviour. If your dog (or bitch) does not wish to mate or be mated, for heaven's sake don't keep trying to persuade them. Virgo is the sign of the Virgin and 'touch-me-not' means exactly what it says. But even though they may be low on sexual drive they're high on the concept of service to others. Watch this too however. We all know of the helpmeet so dedicated to looking after us that they wind up controlling our every thought and action. Unless you're careful your Virgo dog is capable of doing just that. On the other hand he will be dependable and sincere and if you anticipate his weaknesses will make the very best of reliable companions. Not that he altogether lacks subtlety. If he doesn't want to do something he'll probably pretend to be ill. The surest way of checking whether this is genuine is to offer him a bath. Most dogs aren't exactly enamoured of a tub full of lukewarm water and a lot of soap but Virgoans can't get enough. For them cleanliness may not be next to godliness but it's certainly synonymous with happiness. In this, as in most other ways, they set themselves high standards and are supremely self critical whilst, at the same time, strongly resenting criticism from others. Living with a Virgo dog is not dissimilar to living with a maddeningly perfectionist secretary or housekeeper. So long as they have their way they'll run both your lives efficiently and peacefully. But always remember that it's their prerogative to draw attention to any of your shortcomings which may endanger the smooth progress of your co-existence and not the other way around. The slightest fault-finding on your part, however well merited, will strain their patience and upset their morale. So, when acquiring a Virgo dog, just as when engaging a secretary or housekeeper it is wise to lay down your own ground rules firmly at the very start. Once they have been understood and accepted by him and you have appreciated the strengths and limitations of his character there is no reason why the pair of you shouldn't live happily ever after.

DO:
Give him wholesome food on a clean plate at regular hours.
Let him finish every scrap of it.
Bath him till you can't stand it any longer.
Be a shepherd.

Don't leave him with people he doesn't like

DON'T:

Try and mate him when he doesn't want it.

Leave him with people he doesn't like (*never* leave him in quarantine).

Allow him to become over helpful.

Criticize.

MOST COMPATIBLE HUMAN SIGNS:

Taurus, Capricorn, Pisces.

HEALTH:

** Stomach and Intestines.

 * Feet. All minor ailments.

ᒐIBRA

(24th September — 23rd October)

IT'S taken months of arguing with yourself, weighing up the pros and cons, anticipating the best and the worst, but at last you've made up your mind and decided to buy a dog. Not just any dog, what's more. A Yorkshire terrier. You've seen him at one of those large canine emporiums, almost a miniature zoo, and you've put down a deposit in order to reserve him while you spend a couple more sleepless nights wondering whether you've really made the right choice. Weary but finally committed you go to collect him and there he is wagging his tail, delighted to

see you. 'Fancy', says the sales lady encouragingly, 'he knows you already,' and she pats you both with professional approval, cementing the bargain. But you're not looking at either of them. You've noticed a brown and white cocker spaniel pup with long silky ears and a pair of eyes that could melt an iceberg at twenty paces. They're staring straight at you and you're no iceberg. You're just butter.

'I — er — I think I've changed my mind', you mutter, 'I'm not *sure* of course but . . .' The sales lady sighs. She's met your sort before and if she's studied astrology she'll know just what you are. A Libra. In which case you'd better make sure that your dog, be he a Yorkie, a cocker or anything else, is not. If he is you'll spend the rest of your lives in a state of mutual indecision, each feeding upon the growing hesitation of the other, until in the end you'll neither of you do anything for fear of making some irretrievable mistake. If, however, you happen to be an Aquarian or a strong minded Gemini, or almost anything else except a Libran, then by all means share your life with a Libran dog. He will welcome a partner who knows how to make up his mind. It'll save him having to make up his own. Not that he's lazy or stupid, far from it. He's a gentle animal who seeks a pleasant uncomplicated life, dislikes problems, dirt and uncongenial surroundings and always tends to adopt the ideas of a stronger partner. Above all he requires a *balanced* relationship, the feeling that his owner understands him and can communicate with him without difficulty.

IF you don't think you're capable of this or simply haven't got the time the next best thing is to find him a companion in the shape of a second dog, or even a cat — but on no account another Libran like himself. They won't fight because in order to fight it is necessary to quarrel first and this is something of which Librans neither approve nor partake. They also strongly dislike seeing anyone else indulging in it. Beware therefore of getting into an argument with your wife/husband/lover/child in front of such a dog. He will first try to stop you by interposing himself between you and wagging his tail in an enthusiastic but strictly impartial manner. This having failed to achieve the desired result (it usually makes matters worse) he will leap at each of you in turn and attempt to kiss (lick) your faces. The one who is getting the worst of the battle at that moment will probably knock the dog out of the way and the other will call him/her a vicious savage who doesn't deserve to have a pet, let alone a wife/husband. The dog, having realized by now that direct intervention is useless, will start tearing round you in tight circles barking at the top of his lungs in a last attempt to distract you from your contest. This well-meant manoeuvre will come to an abrupt and untimely end when you both boot him out of the

Do buy another cat as a companion

room and slam the door in his face. Such an experience shouldn't happen to any dog and in the case of a Libran will render him highly nervous and may even make him quite ill. Their sign being that of the Scales they have an implicit faith in justice and fair play and when these have clearly miscarried to such a marked degree they tend to become morose, resentful, even bitter. However such moods can be quickly dispelled with a little judicious coaxing. Like the Scales themselves Libran dogs swing rapidly from despair to hope, from lassitude to energy, from down to up. They will always respond to an effort to entertain them. In bad moments try doing your funny imitations, like pretending to bark and wag your tail. They will at once enter into the spirit of the game by giving their rendition of you jumping into your favourite armchair and refusing to budge until someone says that dinner is ready. They enjoy their meals but never make the mistake of offering them a choice of foods. The strenuous effort of deciding which to eat first may prove too much for them to cope with. They are far from ideal as show dogs because of their naturally reticent characters and also because they don't like crowds. By the same token they are not at their best at large cocktail parties, so if you want to display the charm and personality of your Libra dog to your friends do so at small select gatherings, otherwise he may, at best, go and hide in the lavatory, or, at worst, snarl at or even nip the star guest who you're trying to impress with your well organized and smoothly-run home life. This is simply because huge mobile forests of strange legs unnerve them. No Libran dog will ever willingly let you down. On the contrary, once he knows that you understand his ways and are prepared to cooperate, he will do everything he can to please you. Except make up his mind in a hurry.

DO:

Buy another dog or a cat as a companion (providing he's not also a Libra).

Communicate with him in a *balanced* fashion.

Make up your mind whether to go for a walk or stay by the fire (he won't make up his).

Give *small* dinner parties.

DON'T:

Enter him for Crufts.

Quarrel with your wife/husband etc in front of him.

Expect clear cut or rapid decisions.

Be unjust.

MOST COMPATIBLE HUMAN SIGNS:

Gemini, Aquarius, Aries.

HEALTH:

** Skin Troubles. Kidneys.

 * Too many sweets. Emotional Problems.

SCORPIO

(24th October — 22nd November)

THIS is not only the sign of the Scorpion but also that of the Eagle and dogs born under it can be either nasty and spiteful (the Scorpion with the sting) or possessed of beautiful thoughts and high ideals (the Eagle soaring ever upward). More often than not their characters contain a mixture of both resulting in a continual conflict within their natures. This can pose awkward problems for the dog and even more awkward ones for his owner unless he is previously aware of the particular strains and contradictions inherent in the Scorpio make up. Whether they be good or bad, constructive or destructive, gentle or aggressive, full of love or barbed with hate, Scorpio feelings are always intense and passionate. For example, you ask if you may bring your Scorpio dog with you to friends for the weekend. They haven't yet met him but you assure them that he is well trained, has impeccable manners, takes to strangers, is gentle with children and will get on like a house on fire with their elderly bitch, Bessie. Of course they agree, particularly since Bessie has long ago been rendered infertile. It will be great fun for her to have a companion to play with, they say, she'll feel young again. Scorpio arrives and lives up to all his publicity, making friends all round, enchanting the children, the perfect canine house guest. Then he meets Bessie and in the twinkling of an eye friendship is replaced by passion, good manners by naked sexual desire. In so many words, he attempts without hesitation and with burning ardour, to rape her. You try to save the day by repeating Noel Coward's joke about poor Bessie going suddenly blind and kindly Scorpio pushing her all the way to St Dunstans, but it is too late. Bessie, like Queen Victoria is not amused and wastes no time in making her feelings crystal clear. His suit summarily dismissed, his pride humiliated, Scorpio changes abruptly from gallant guest into a vindictive, quarrelsome and altogether impossible intruder. Sexual rejection has transformed him from jolly Jekyll into horrible Hyde. He is not really to blame. He can't help his nature. But the weekend has started on the slippery path towards ruin. That night you lecture your dog on his bad behaviour and he sits obediently in the corner of the room, apparently drinking in every word, but actually nursing his secret plans for revenge. Next day you all take both dogs for a walk and whilst Bessie is allowed to run free, Scorpio is kept on a leash until your host begs that he be set free. He is quite sure, he says, that the nice dog won't repeat his unfortunate advances and, as Scorpio could tell him, he's damn right. He wouldn't touch the silly bitch with a barge pole. He has a darker and far more appropriate fate in store for her. He frisks round her inviting her to join him in a gallop across the field and eventually the elderly Bessie falls for it. Off they go to the general relief and approval of all the humans present, Scorpio leading by a length and gradually increasing the pace. Only he is aware of the fate towards which he is leading her and he has planned its denouement with all the cunning and foresight of a Napoleon. At precisely the right moment he leaps into the air, clearing a wet and steaming pile of manure as though it were Becher's Brook. Bessie, taken by surprise not only fails to leap but plunges straight on into the evil-smelling trap. Scorpio returns to your side wagging his tail and awaiting congratulations. It is no concern of his that the weekend is now beyond redemption. His honour has been satisfied. Do not imagine from the foregoing that Scorpio dogs should automatically be left behind when visiting acquaintances in the country or anywhere else. Far from it.

I T is only when they feel threatened or insulted that they react by exhibiting the baser and more unfortunate side of their nature. The other side includes a great many virtues. They are intensely loyal to their friends and owners, always seeking to improve and refine their relationships, and, like the elephant, never, never forgetting a kindness. Equally, on the reverse side once more, they never forget an injury or injustice either. They are fiercely possessive of what they consider to be their own property and woe betide any other dog or human who attempts to remove it from them, be it a bone or the special piece of old felt on which they have elected to sleep. In short, Scorpios, like the rest of us, can be saints or sinners, perhaps tending by virtue of their passionate natures, to go a bit further in both directions than most. It is up to you to brave the occasional spikiness and stings and to seek out the gentleness, creativity and charm. If you succeed in so doing you will be amply rewarded by the loyalty and friendship of your Scorpio dog.

DO:
Make allowances for the fact that there is a constant war going on within his own nature.
Permit him an active sex life.
Appreciate the intensity of his feelings.
Put up with the odd bouts of snappiness (which won't last long) and enjoy the affection and true comradeship (which will).

DON'T:
Allow yourself to be put off by his moments of inscrutability.
Choose the wrong bitch/dog for him/her.

Don't allow yourself to be put off by his moments of inscrutability

Worry if he suddenly changes his life style for reasons which are not immediately apparent to you.
Ever imagine that he will forget either a kind word or a cruel one.

MOST COMPATIBLE HUMAN SIGNS:
Cancer, Pisces, Taurus.

HEALTH:

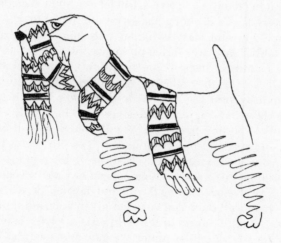

** Nose and Throat.
 * Circulation. Sexual Organs. Varicose veins.

47

SAGITTARIUS

(23rd November — 22nd December)

IS your life dull? Do you wake each morning only to ponder mournfully how you're going to fill in time till the television begins? Is every day a dreary repetition of the one before? Are you a slave to routine? Do you sometimes feel you could murder your wife/husband if she/he says just *once* more 'see you this evening darling, have a good day'? Do you occasionally feel an urge to scream and break up the furniture? If your answer to any of the above questions is in the affirmative you should seriously consider getting a Sagittarian dog. If they all are you should drop everything else and call the nearest kennels right away. Unless, that is, you happen to be a bore. Most people don't know whether they are or not and, as with halitosis, it is unlikely that even their best friends will enlighten them. A Sagittarian dog will and without delay. They cannot abide bores and will so inform you in no uncertain terms. But let us assume that although you are bored, you do not actually bore others. Okay — buy a Sagittarian dog and start living, if not dangerously, at least unpredictably. They are eternal optimists, full of jokes, versatile, and, like Geminis, detest being tied down to a routine. Half horse, half Archer, they take life at a full gallop, shooting their arrows joyfully into the air and letting them fall where they may. A walk with a Sagittarian dog ceases to be simply exercise or a means of getting from A to B and becomes a full-blooded adventure, a mystery tour crammed with exciting possibilities. Suppose your intention was merely to stroll down to the village shop in order to buy some washing powder or a pack of cigarettes, something you've been doing day in and day out for years. Your dog will change all that. You've never given a second thought to that horse cropping grass in the field on your left. At least not until Sagittarius scrambles under the gate and starts barking at him. Alarmed, you yell at him to come back. He takes no notice. He is far too busy making rapid darts at the horse in the manner

48

of a friendly four-legged matador attempting to arouse the
interest of a bull. You climb anxiously over the gate, calling his
name but it's too late. The owner of the horse, your local farmer,
is approaching from the far side of the field and, horror of
horrors, the horse is now cantering after the dog who is weaving
a crazy zig-zag pattern across the grass. The farmer stumps
purposefully towards you and out of the corner of your eye you
observe that the horse is now galloping with the dog running at
full stretch beside him like an eager greyhound slipped from the
traps. You wait helplessly for the first blast of the farmer's wrath
but it never materializes. Instead he grins and says that what his
old mare needed was a bit of exercise. She was getting fat and
now that his son has gone off to work in London, the damn fool,
there's no one to ride her any more. Suddenly the sun is brighter,
the air more sparkling and you feel younger than you've felt for
years. You used to ride you hear yourself saying, could you
perhaps help out? The deal is struck and your life is altered.
Three days a week you ride the mare and your dog runs happily
beside you. Sagittarians are like that. Because they really believe
that each new day will present a new opportunity, so it comes to
pass. They are optimists and luck favours the dog (or man) who

believes in it. But your new horse life is not all. You have achieved a pleasantly intimate relationship with the village shop and all because your dog has noticed a small side of bacon on the shelf above the refrigerator and leapt up and stolen it. With tears in his eyes the shopkeeper tells you that this is exactly what *his* dog used to do before he was run over, God rest his soul, by one of those damned tourists in their blasted motor cars. It's high time, as he keeps telling his wife, that they bought another, and seeing yours jump up and pinch that bacon has been like a timely prompting from above. Dazed, you offer to pay for it and are refused. Tomorrow there'll be a juicy bone on that same shelf so be sure to bring him again. Of course you know that your Sagittarian was simply being unforgiveably greedy (they often are) but once again his forthrightness and positive thinking has paid off.

Do try living on a farm

THEY are not only greedy for food. Their ardent natures can never receive too much love and affection. But whilst they are tolerant and easy-going their very frankness and openness can sometimes take the form of supreme tactlessness. This is often because, although capable of planning and appreciating vast projects, they dislike the finicky details involved in bringing them to fruition. They are, for instance, quite hopeless at Christmas when relatives bring beautifully wrapped and labelled gifts for the whole family and deposit them carefully beneath the tree to await the opening ceremony. Your dog will open his and, if possible, eat it long before the Day has dawned and, since he cannot read, may also open others not intended for him before discovering his error. This does not make for the happiest of starts to Christmas morning.

A Sagittarian dog usually lives to an advanced age and retains his full faculties, energy and *joie de vivre* right to the end. So unless you are sure you'll be able to keep pace with him for a long, long time it's better not to start at all. But if you can you'll rarely have another dull moment.

DO:
Develop a sense of adventure.
Try living on a farm.
Expect the unexpected.
Have confidence in him even when you haven't the faintest idea what he's doing or why he's doing it.

DON'T:
Be a bore.
Live in the middle of a town.
Expect a quiet life.
Think that just because your energy may diminish with age, his will too. It won't.

MOST COMPATIBLE HUMAN SIGNS:
Aries, Leo, Gemini.

HEALTH:
** Accidents. Hiccoughs. Legs.
 * Liver or lung troubles.

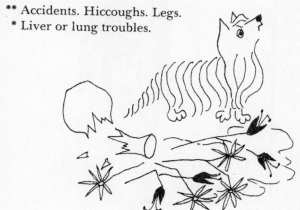

51

CAPRICORN

(23rd December — 19th January)

THE majority of dogs born under this sign also enjoy their later years the best when the fevers of earlier life are stilled. But that is about all they have in common with Sagittarians. Capricorn is the sign of the Goat yet there is little that is goatlike about Capricornians in the generally accepted sense of the word. They are endowed with a practical down-to-earth mentality, all four feet are firmly planted on the ground and, although they are willing to accept discipline for their own betterment, they do not enjoy remaining in a subordinate

position for longer than is absolutely necessary. You could assume from this that they would make ideal show dogs and you might well be right but before you rush off to enter yours for Crufts do please remember one all important fact. The only place worth achieving for a Capricorn is the first. To come in second is no different from coming in last because both spell failure and failure will almost certainly result in an acute attack of depression. So, if you're not pretty sure that yours has a better than even chance of emerging as Top Dog you'd better stay away not only from Crufts but the show at your local village hall as well. That is unless you are fully prepared to cope with his depression and coax him out of it by persuading him that next time he'll surely make it as Champion of Champions. Do that and his ambition will do the rest. The gloom will be dispelled and he'll cooperate with you in attaining for himself the one position he cherishes above all others — that at the very top. You'll need patience because he won't be hurried but once you've helped him to overcome his limitations and convinced him that the golden prize is an actual possibility, there's no reason why, with a bit of luck, you shouldn't both make the front pages of the national dailies. But before such euphoric honours can be considered you'll have to take great care of him, particularly in puppyhood when he'll be prone to illnesses, notably afflictions of the skin. If you think he's got fleas disinfect him at once. Too much scratching can lead to unpleasant rashes. As he grows up these physical threats to his well-being will diminish but a moral one may take their place — that of snobbery. Capricorn dogs don't exactly suffer from superiority complexes. They just know they *are* superior. This can lead to unpopularity in their social lives. Dogs who think they're better than other dogs are apt to get a bad name and if they persist in their 'I am His Majesty's Dog from Kew, pray tell me sir who's dog are you' attitude, may become ostracized, outcasts. This separation from the common herd won't worry them in the very least but if carried to sufficient lengths may well worry you. Take for instance, his attitude to those communal meeting places of all dogs, the local trees and lamp posts. They visit them as we would visit the local pub, not only for purposes of relief, but to keep in touch with what's going on in the neighbourhood, sniff out who's new in town. At least run of the mill plebeian dogs do. But not some Capricorns. I once heard of a London flat dweller who owned a well brought up and impeccably trained dachshund. His manners were above reproach in every respect save one.

Prone to mental depression

ON returning from a walk he always peed against a hat stand which stood in the hall. This drove his owner almost to the point of insanity until he realized that his dachshund would risk a stricture (like Geminians for opposite reasons) rather than pass water on any of the assorted uprights along their route which were in constant use by other less socially distinguished dogs of the district. He finally solved the problem by planting a shrub next to a drain on his small balcony and yelling 'outside!' at his Capricornian companion as soon as they got inside the front door. This was an example of dire necessity becoming the mother of invention but in less immediately dramatic circumstances it is unwise to allow a Capricorn dog to dictate to you. Once he realizes that he's got the upper hand he'll never relinquish it and you'll find that he's running your life instead of sharing it. His motives for this aren't really bad — it's simply that he can't help enjoying power and is sufficiently pragmatic to realize when he's got it. The trick is to allow him to experience it in ways which are designed to serve you rather than dominate you. For instance, the telephone or front door ploy. When either bell rings pretend you're a bit deaf and haven't heard it. He'll bark, and if that doesn't work, start pulling at your sleeve. You should then look round in surprise, clasp your hand to your forehead as though receiving a revelation from above, and praise him warmly for being so clever and alert. He'll bask in his sense of power and achievement and as you pick up the phone or answer the door his expression will clearly denote his satisfaction that luckily, thank God, there's at least *one* person in the place who isn't an idiot.

He is, let's face it, a social climber and you, of course, are not. But occasionally you may have cause to visit rather grand friends who are still able to afford not only a country mansion but the staff to go with it. As the owner of a Capricorn dog you need no longer fear the look of snooty pity on the butler's face as he takes your battered suitcase from the car. Your dog will have already upstaged him by entering the chateau as though he owned it and your host will be fully occupied in greeting him as one aristocrat to another. He will accept his welcome as a right but if he could speak he would undoubtedly be saying in a satisfied aside 'That's fixed that bloody butler.'

Capricorn dogs will always keep you on your toes and, once you've come to terms with their insatiable lust for power and position, can be the most stimulating of all canine companions.

DO:
Show him — providing you're sure he'll win First Prize.
Be careful of illnesses when he's a puppy, particularly afflictions of the skin.
Recognize that he can't help being a snob. He was born one.
Allow him to *think* he's running the joint.

DON'T:
Praise him for getting second prize. It will do nothing to cheer him.
Try to hurry him.
Leave him behind when you're visiting a Stately Home.
Allow him to *actually* run the joint.

MOST COMPATIBLE HUMAN SIGNS:
Taurus, Virgo, Cancer.

HEALTH:
** Skin allergies and infections. Knees.
 * Mental depression.

AQUARIUS

(20th January — 19th February)

IF you want a dog purely as a sort of love object, something on which to lavish affection, pet pamper and cosset at all hours, do not make the mistake of buying an Aquarian one. Over-possessiveness will make him feel he's being stifled, suffocated. This doesn't mean he's naturally unfriendly, simply that he instinctively mistrusts and feels embarrassed by ostentatious displays of emotion and prefers to keep his essential self to himself. Most Aquarius dogs can be likened to good stockbrokers. They are amiable but cautious, think a great deal about the future, possess considerable powers of intuition, and may sometimes behave as though they were four-legged computers. They also have a penchant for joining organizations, particularly those with humanitarian aims and if you can find one with a good memory (many Aquarians have poor ones) he might well make an excellent seeing eye dog. He won't form a close relationship in a hurry but once you've proved yourself worthy of his attention he'll become completely loyal and never let you down. In addition, his own feelings of self-sufficiency and self-assurance will transmit themselves to you and although he may sometimes appear to be detached and distant this will only be because he is busy weighing up a situation whilst taking care not to allow his judgement to become impaired by emotional involvements.

For the normally sighted owner however, this peculiarly Aquarian desire to become part of a larger group can also have more troublesome aspects. Imagine for example that you want to take a long, quiet contemplative stroll in order to wrestle with some tricky problem of your own. Take an Aquarian dog along and you won't have a chance of solving it. He'll either disappear altogether in order to play with his own gang of canine friends thus causing you to waste precious time searching for him, or bring the whole lot to join you in your walk with the result that

your hoped-for peaceful progress will be marred by a ceaseless cacophony of barks and so many strange animals will become entangled with your feet that you'll feel like a reluctant Noah leading his unwieldy flock towards some remote Ark. He can create even worse havoc by insisting that you meet the owners of his circle of friends. His most effective method of achieving this is to follow them closely in whatever direction they happen to be going whilst completely ignoring your increasingly frantic requests to return to your side. Eventually you will be compelled to approach the unknown owners in order physically to detach him from their presence while feebly muttering apologies for what is, in fact, his lack of manners but looks uncomfortably like your own total inability to control him. If such owners happen to be attractive members of the opposite sex these cunningly arranged introductions can have their good points but if you are busily engaged in trying to work out how the devil you're going to pay your income tax or placate a temporarily estranged wife or husband, you may not be in the best mood to take proper advantage of them. But do not despair. It could be a lot worse. At least you'll be spared the necessity of rescuing him from

Don't smother him with affection

fights. Aquarian dogs are simply not geared for battles. They realize that in an imperfect world such warlike encounters must have their place but they prefer to leave them to others. They are not necessarily against all forms of violence but have no intention whatsoever of becoming involved in them. This does not mean that they are entirely docile or malleable. Far from it. Their obstinacy can match that of the most obdurate mule any day and, since they are considerably more intelligent, they'll probably end up not only by getting their own way but also by proving to their own satisfaction, if not to yours, that they are the only ones who are really in step. The fact that they tend to live constantly in the future combined with their intuitive abilities will often provide them with astonishingly accurate premonitions.

THESE can be extremely useful as for instance when they refuse point blank to enter a strange hotel which later catches on fire and is burnt to the ground or, on a less dramatic note, proves to be infested with bed bugs. On the other hand they can be extremely irritating, as, for example, when they take a rooted objection to the girl/boy friend you're hoping to chat up as a prelude to a more intimate relationship in the privacy of your car. Your loyal Aquarian dog, *knowing* that this particular romantic attachment must end in disaster sooner or later, and wishing to spare you as much misery as possible, will take appropriate steps to nip it in the bud there and then. He will either secrete himself in the car and wait quietly on the back seat until the time comes to make his unexpected presence known, or, failing this, will follow it until it comes to rest in some quiet country lane and then hurl himself breathlessly through the open window, landing muddily between you and your paramour at what can best be described as *le moment critique*. You certainly won't appreciate this intervention but do keep your temper and try not to chastise him because later, when the future has become the present, you'll more than likely have cause to be grateful to him. Always remember that Aquarian dogs live in the days to come rather than the ones that are already at hand and this will help you to understand the apparent contradictions in their characters and enjoy more fully their varied and very real charms.

DO:
Allow him to join canine clubs.
Trust his intuitive judgements.
Respect his inbuilt pacifism.
Remember that whereas you're living today, he's living to-morrow.

DON'T:
Allow him to make you honorary president of the above clubs.
Smother him with affection.
Disregard his premonitions.
Worry if he sometimes appears to be living on another plane of existence.

MOST COMPATIBLE HUMAN SIGNS:
Gemini, Libra, Aries, Leo.

HEALTH:
** Too much cold in winter. Too much heat in summer.
 * Weak ankle bones. Poor circulation.

PISCES

(20th February — 21st March)

WHILST Aquarians imagine the world as it will be, those born under the sign of the Fishes dream of it as it should be, and, if dogs wore spectacles, Piscean pups would see life through those of the rose-coloured variety and continue so to do until their dying day. They are kindly dogs, full of deep feelings, sensitive, of a gentle disposition, easily moved. Whilst ever

60

anxious to help anyone in trouble they will always try to avoid it themselves, or, more simply, conveniently deny its very existence. Anything for a quiet and peaceful life could be their motto and they will adapt themselves to whatever circumstances and company in which they may find themselves in order to achieve it. This seemingly unimpeachable attitude can, if carried to extremes, lead to serious trouble. It is not a good idea to leave

Prone to listlessness

your Piscean dog to look after the empty house whilst you're out at the cinema. If hungry-looking squatters arrive he will show them straight to the food cupboard and, should they start to yawn after their meal, will immediately conduct them to the best bedroom (yours). Burglars, providing they have the sense to realize they are dealing with a Piscean, may expect his full cooperation in return for not being shouted at, or, worse still, physically threatened. On the other hand, these dogs have vast and prolific imaginations and, on seeing the light of a torch flickering first upon one window and then another, may experience the hallucination that Martians have landed and run yowling through the back door in order to hide in whatever undergrowth is available until the threat of extra terrestrial invasion has finally receded. Requests to the local policeman to help find them may be met with a certain lack of enthusiasm particularly if he was the bearer of the torch in the first instance. In terms of more ordinary day to day existence this overriding desire for a placid life can also lead them into the paths of downright deceit, particularly as their abiding concern with the necessity of never being concerned sometimes gives rise to nervous digestive ailments. On such occasions your friendly vet will gladly prescribe the appropriate pills but your psychic (and potentially paranoic) Piscean will resist taking them, not because he dislikes the taste but because some inner Voice has warned him that if he does he may run the danger of becoming addicted. (Before dismissing this as a far out fancy it is wise to remember that Pisceans actually are unusually susceptible to drug poisoning.) In any event your dog is now faced with a dilemma. If he refuses the pills you will become angry, if he swallows them he will become an addict. Either way the tranquillity of his existence will be shattered. There is only one course open to him and he takes it by conning you into believing that he has digested them whereas he has actually stored them in his cheeks or under his tongue until he can find a suitably secret place wherein to dispose of them. The success of this deception will induce a feeling of calm satisfaction and his digestive troubles will probably disappear of their own accord. Thus everyone will be happy, not least the vet who will have received your cheque for his expert advice and treatment.

By now you will have appreciated that there are two distinctly different aspects to your Piscean dog. Depending on one's point of view they are either infuriatingly bland with no real opinions of their own and always ready to take the line of least resistance, or they are understanding, cooperative companions, full of gentleness and genuine generosity. Both are true to a greater or lesser extent and each is symbolized by the two fishes of their sign, one swimming upstream against the current, the other down. They have good memories but they rely on their intuitive sixth sense rather than worldly experience to make decisions, always feeling as opposed to thinking.

THERE is something of the actor in all of them but they are not ambitious and dislike any form of competition. Do not, therefore, waste your time in trying to train them for shows or even expect them to shine in impromptu races with other dogs. But if you're looking for a comparatively quiet and trouble free relationship with an affectionate and pleasant companion and are possessed of sufficient imagination to comprehend and not be thrown by the strange, romantic and unpredictable fantasies which sometimes overtake him in the emotional stream in which he swims, then a Piscean is the dog for you.

DO:
Appreciate that he's a dreamer and make allowances for it.

Realize that he's subject to unknown fears and psychic influences.
Try auto suggestion before trying the vet.
Keep your temper.

DON'T:
Expect him to have strong (or even definite) opinions of his own.
Leave him to guard the house.
Ever attempt to show him.
Think he's going to win a gold medal (or even a bronze) in the local canine olympics.

MOST COMPATIBLE HUMAN SIGNS:
Cancer, Scorpio, Virgo.

HEALTH:
** Colds. Digestive troubles. Paws.
 * Lungs. Listlessness.

DOGS THEN

Where appropriate two possible birth signs are suggested for each dog mentioned in this chapter — but you may have your own ideas.

In his book *Dogs of China and Japan in Nature and Art*, V.W.F. Collier writes of T'ao Hua (Peach Flower), a dog given to the Emperor T'ai-tsung of the Sung Dynasty at the end of the tenth century A.D. 'It was extremely small and very intelligent. It followed the Emperor everywhere but when they went into the Hall of Audience it changed places and walked in front so

that it could announce the arrival of its Imperial Master. T'ai-tsung fell ill and the dog refused to eat; when the Emperor died it manifested its sorrow with tears and whining. The palace eunuchs tried to train Peach Flower to precede the new Emperor into Audience but without success, so the newcomer gracefully bowed out and caused an iron cage to be made with white cushions as a sign of mourning, and this, containing the dog, was carried in the Imperial chair to his master's tomb. There the dog died.'

AQUARIUS or LEO?

Centuries later another canine companion of royalty showed his devotion in a distinctly more active fashion:

Prince Rupert's constant companion during his Civil War campaigns was a poodle by the name of Boye. The Royalist soldiers called him Serjeant-Major-General Boye and their enemies, the Parliamentarians, genuinely believed that he was Rupert's familiar, crediting him with supernatural powers as witness this Roundhead tract written by someone signing himself T.B.

'He is weapon proof himself and probably hath made his Master so too. He salutes and kisseth the Prince, as close as any Christian woman would, and the Prince salutes and kisses him back again as favorily as he would (I will not say any Alderman's wife, but) any Court-Lady as is as little offended with his Breathing. Then they lye perpetually in one bed, sometimes the Prince upon the Dogg and sometimes the Dogg upon the Prince; and what this may in time produce none but the close Committee can tell. That is no Dogg but a witch, a Sorceresse, an enemy to Parliament, that is to Church and State, a Malignant Cavalier Dogg that hath something of Divell in or about him.' The faithful Boye, having slipped the collar which held him in safety, followed his master into battle at Marston Moor. His small body was found amongst those others who had given their lives upon that field.

PISCES or ARIES?
(Prince Rupert was a SAGITTARIAN)

Incidentally Oliver Cromwell had a dog to whom he, or someone with a similar lack of humour, gave the inauspicious name of Coffin Nail.

The name of Isaac Newton's dog aptly reflected the brilliance of his master's intellect. But Diamond was guilty of knocking over a candle, thus setting fire to a pile of papers and effectively destroying 'the almost finished labours of some years'. Even in the face of this catastrophe the great man's celebrated patience did not entirely desert him, producing a remarkably mild reproof: 'Oh Diamond! Diamond! Thou little knowest the mischief done!'

TAURUS or GEMINI?
(Sir Isaac Newton was a CAPRICORN)

A dog who probably never knocked over anything and whose character resembled more that of a ministering angel than any form of devil was Elizabeth Barrett Browning's beloved spaniel, Flush.

> But of *thee* it shall be said,
> This dog watched beside a bed
> Day and night unweary,
> Watched within a curtained room,
> Where no sunbeam broke the gloom
> Round the sick and dreary.
>
> Roses, gathered for a vase,
> In that chamber died apace,
> Beam and breeze resigning —
> This dog only, waited on,
> Knowing that when light is gone,
> Love remains for shining.
>
> Other dogs in thymy dew
> Tracked the hares and followed through
> Sunny moor or meadow —

This dog only, crept and crept
Next a languid cheek that slept,
Sharing in the shadow.

Other dogs of loyal cheer
Bounded at the whistle clear,
Up the woodside hieing —
This dog only, watched in reach
Of a faintly uttered speech,
Or a louder sighing.

VIRGO or PISCES?
(Elizabeth Browning was a PISCES)

Many writers have been dog lovers and have chosen to record the fact. Perhaps they found, as many still do, that canine companionship, silent but steadfast, assists in lessening the essential loneliness of their task. The Holloway home for lost dogs (forerunner of the present one at Battersea) was established in 1860 and met with much criticism and mockery from the press and public. No less an acute social observer than Charles Dickens took up the cudgels on their behalf. In his journal 'All the Year Round' dated 2nd August 1862, he wrote a graphic and moving article called 'Two Dog Shows' in which he compared a visit to the Prize Dog Show at the Islington Hall (forerunner of the present Crufts) with the one only half a mile away at Holloway. 'At Islington . . . all was prosperity. Here, all is adversity . . . At Islington there were dogs estimated by their owners at hundreds of pounds. Here there are animals that are, only from a humane point of view, worth the drop of prussic acid which puts them out of their misery . . . If people really think it wrong to spend a very, very little money on that poor cur whose face I frankly own often haunts my memory . . . let them leave it to its fate; but I think it somewhat hard that they should turn the whole scheme into ridicule, or assail it with open ferocity as a dangerous competitor with other enterprises for public favour . . . It is . . . an extraordinary monument of the remarkable affection with which English people regard the race of dogs; an evidence of that hidden fund of feeling which survives in some hearts even the rough ordeal of London life in the nineteenth century.'

And still does, thanks to their equally devoted successors at Battersea, in the twentieth.

Twenty-five years earlier Dickens had spoken in lighter vein of a particular dog in the second chapter of *Pickwick Papers*. It belonged (or so he claimed) to the redoubtable Mr. Jingle. 'Ah! you should keep dogs — fine animals — sagacious creatures — dog of my own once — Pointer — surprising instinct — out shooting one day — entering enclosure — whistled — dog stopped — whistled again — Ponto — no go: stock still — called him — Ponto, Ponto — wouldn't move — dog transfixed — staring at a board — looked up, saw an inscription — "Gamekeeper has orders to shoot all dogs found in this inclosure" — wouldn't pass it — wonderful dog — valuable dog that — very.'

CANCER or AQUARIUS?

Thomas Carlyle, historian, philosopher, author of *The French Revolution* owned a dog called Nero but did *not* love it. Fortunately his wife, Jane, did. 'It is,' she wrote in 1849, twenty-three years after their marriage, 'really a comfort to have something alive and cheery and fond of me, always there.' This statement possibly derived from the fact that Mr Carlyle was never really fond of anyone other than himself. Even Queen Victoria thought him 'strange looking, eccentric' with a 'drawling melancholy voice', holding forth 'upon the utter degradation of everything'. Nero had lived with the Carlyles at their house in Cheyne Row for less than a year when, perhaps sharing the views of the Queen Empress, he suddenly jumped from the library window, over the street railings, onto the pavement below. Mrs Carlyle was still in bed when she heard the servants crying out 'Oh God! Oh Nero!' and immediately sprang up and rushed down the stairs. Thomas came from his bedroom with soap all over his chin and asked 'Has anything happened to Nero?' 'Oh sir,' a servant answered, 'he *must* have broken all his legs, he leaped out at *your* window!' 'God bless me,' Carlyle replied and returned to finish his shaving. In spite of this incident Nero survived for another ten years and in 1857 Jane said of him: 'Carlyle delights in torturing him, which he calls playing with him. He snaps the tongs at him and Nero does not like that. He once even tied an empty can to his tail and sent the poor dog scampering all over the house in great terror. It was cruel of him to do that — absolutely cruel — and I told him so. I told him it was an amusement unfit for a philosopher — low, degrading.' Carlyle responded by laughing at her and at Nero. 'But,' his wife added with understandable satisfaction, 'he did not do it again'. At the age of eleven Nero was run over by a cart and his mistress wrote of his dying moments: 'I *could* not lift him . . . but I kissed his poor little head — and *he licked my cheek*. Then I ran and shut myself into my bedroom and flung myself down and cried — as I hadn't cried since I was a girl'. Even Thomas Carlyle, who had earlier recommended 'a little Prussic acid' for the ailing Nero, admitted to finding himself 'quite unexpectedly and distractedly torn to pieces by the memory of the thing'. Several years later Mrs Carlyle, now in failing health, sought companionship and solace in another pet. She went for a drive with her new 'little dog' and let it out for a run. It was knocked down by another carriage and she leapt out, rescued it and returned with it to her own which then drove on. When it stopped again Jane Carlyle was found sitting with folded hands — dead.

SCORPIO or SAGITTARIUS?
(Thomas Carlyle was a SAGITTARIUS).

Another window jumping dog with literary connections was Sir Walter Scott's Maida, who leapt not away from his master but towards him in over enthusiastic greeting as he approached up the drive at Abbotsford. Unfortunately the window in question was closed at the time and Lady Scott thought the dog must be mad and wished a servant to shoot him. But Scott, unlike Carlyle, knew that his dog loved him and answered: 'Maida shall not be shot; no, not if he broke every window in the place'. Some time later, on October 22nd 1824, he wrote from Abbotsford: 'Old Maida died quietly in his straw last week, after a good supper, which, considering his weak state, was rather a deliverance. He is buried below his monument'. And he was surely thinking of Maida when he paid this fine tribute: 'The Almighty, who gave the dog to be the companion of our pleasures and toils, hath invested him with a nature noble and incapable of deceit . . . . He has a share of man's intelligence but no share of man's falsehood.

You may bribe an assassin to slay a man, or a witness to take his life by false accusation, but you cannot make a dog tear his benefactor. He is the friend of man . . .'

LEO or ARIES?

(Scott was a LEO)

The young Byron felt much the same. He described his Newfoundland, Boatswain, as 'the Phoenix of canine quadrupeds'. He had acquired him as a puppy and after his death in 1808 Byron wrote to Francis Hodgson 'Boatswain is to be buried in a vault waiting for myself. I have also written an epitaph, which I would send were it not for two reasons: one is that it is too long for a letter; and the other, that I hope you will someday read it on the spot where it will be engraved . . .'

This is that epitaph inscribed on Boatswain's tomb in the garden at Newstead Abbey: 'Near this spot are deposited the remains of one who possessed beauty without vanity, strength without insolence, courage without ferocity, and all the virtues of man without his vices. This praise, which would be unmeaning flattery if inscribed over human ashes, is but a just tribute to the memory of Boatswain, a dog who was born in Newfoundland in May 1803 and died at Newstead, November 18th 1808.'

In his Will of 1809 Byron specified that the monument over his dog was not to be disturbed when he was laid beside it.

Evidently a TAURUS or a GEMINI?

Alexander Pope who owned a succession of Great Danes and named each one, regardless of sex, Bounce, did not trouble himself with such grandiloquent epitaphs. A lady Bounce was entrusted to Lord Orrery under whose care she died:

'Ah Bounce! Ah gentle beast! Why wouldst thou dye
When thou hadst Meat enough, and Orrery?'

However commemorated the death of a beloved dog is always a matter of great sadness to the owner who is left behind.

Some of their feelings are recorded on the small headstones in Hyde Park's dog cemetry. 'Darling Dolly. My Sunbeam. My consolation. My love. 1892-1898'. 'GRIT. Loved and Lost February 21st 1900. Could I think we'd meet again, it would lessen half my pain'. And a harsher echo of our own sterner days: 'Prince Marine Commando of Anisor. K.C. Reg: No: 13991/67. He asked for so little and gave so much'. Another inscription, commendably untheatrical, reads simply: 'Darling Fluff 1895'. It marks the grave of Sir Henry Irving's fox

terrier. This little cemetery began, literally, by accident. In 1880 a dog belonging to the Duchess of Cambridge was run over and killed in the Bayswater Road. Her Grace, distraught with grief, carried its body through the Victoria Gate into Hyde Park and had it buried there and then.

On the other side of the Atlantic such events are frequently ordered rather differently. Death, like so much of life, is big business. In her book *Petishism*, Kathleen Szasz speaks of an exclusive Garden of Rest run by the Animal Funeral Home Inc. whose brochure offers 'a new, desirable elevation in animal service'. She continues: 'The dead pet is picked up in a white station wagon whose driver is instructed to handle the corpse with due reverence. At the funeral parlour it is groomed and placed on a bier in the position it was wont to lie in when alive, until the owner and the human *and animal friends* (my italics) have paid their last respects. People for whom only the best is good enough can get the "preferred service", conducted from one of the "slumber rooms" opening out of the softly lit lounge and with piped in music. There are special "slumber rooms" for each pet species . . . the colour and furnishings harmonizing with the breed and character of the dear departed.'

In case that that isn't enough to spur you into reserving a slumber room for your favourite pooch right now, Ms Szasz adds the following from the American magazine *Dog's World*: 'In the shocked silence that followed the death of Abraham Lincoln, one of the generals at his bedside uttered an unforgettable phrase: 'Now he belongs to the ages'. We can only paraphrase this utterance at the news of the death of Ch: Phidgity Snow Dream'. One cannot help wondering what unforgettable animal noises Phidgity Snow Dream's canine friends may have uttered as they filed past the bier on which the departed champ lay as he was wont to lie when alive.

Being compared to a President in death is one thing but a shaggy Airedale by the name of Laddie Boy actually shared the corridors of power with one during his lifetime. Laddie Boy not only personally delivered the newspapers to his ex-newspaper-man master, President Warren Harding, but also attended Cabinet meetings seated in a chair specially provided for him. He was instrumental in defeating a House of Representatives motion to save money by doing away with the United States Marine Band at White House social functions. James Henry MacLafferty (Republican, California) asked the House which they preferred: 'The President keeping his Marine Band music or listening to Laddie Boy racing around the White House grounds, howling, with a tomato can tied to his tail?' There is no evidence that the President was ever guilty of tying anything to Laddie Boy's tail but the Marine Band won the day. A statuette of Laddie Boy now stands in the Smithsonian.

CAPRICORN or LIBRA?

(President Harding was a SCORPIO).

Forty years later another dog sat in on White House Cabinet meetings. His name was Yuki and he belonged to President Lyndon B. Johnson (who had already shocked dog lovers of the world by lifting up Yuki's predecessors, the beagles Him and Her, by their ears). Yuki was a mongrel who had been found wandering in Austin, Texas, and when Mr Johnson was asked why he was so devoted to him, he replied 'He speaks with a Texas accent and he likes me'. The second reason, at least, seems immediately understandable but even so, Yuki, unlike Laddie Boy, sat *under* the Cabinet table.

LIBRA or ARIES?

Laddie Boy may have reprieved the United States Marine Band but a bulldog by the name of Dan achieved possibly even greater immortality by providing the inspiration for a truly great piece

of music. He belonged to George Robertson Sinclair, a close friend of Sir Edward Elgar and one time organist at Hereford Cathedral. Dan used to attend chorus rehearsals in the Cathedral and growl when people sang out of tune. Elgar, who had been forced to part with his own dog, Scap, when he married (Lady Elgar did not like dogs), was fascinated by Dan and his exploits. One day when he was walking with Sinclair beside the Wye, Dan fell into the river and eventually managed to scramble out again.

'Set that to music,' Sinclair said.

In a note on Number xi of his Enigma Variations Elgar wrote: 'I did: here it is . . . the variation . . . has nothing to do with organs or cathedrals, or, except remotely, with G.R.S. The first few bars were suggested by his great bulldog Dan (a well known character) falling down the steep bank of the river Wye (bar one); his paddling up stream to find a landing place (bars two and three); and his rejoicing bark on landing (second half of bar five).'

SAGITTARIUS or VIRGO?
(Sir Edward Elgar was a GEMINI.)

Some notable dogs have spent considerably more of their lives in or on the water than the inspirational Dan. One such was Judy, a pedigree pointer born into the chaos of Shanghai in 1936 and enrolled in the Royal Navy whilst still a puppy as a member of the crew of the gunboat, H.M.S. Gnat, complete with an official service number, an open top box and a regulation blanket. The original intention had been to train her as a gundog for shooting parties ashore during off duty periods but the fact that everyone on board regarded her as a much loved pet, combined with the tide of events, precluded this. She narrowly escaped drowning after falling overboard in the Yangtse and when the Gnat's ship's company were transferred to H.M.S. Grasshopper Judy went with them and saw action on board before the fall of Singapore, acting as a valuable and accurate early warning system by barking in the direction of approaching enemy planes before they actually appeared. In spite of this the Grasshopper was sunk by bombing in 1942 and Judy and the other survivors were marooned on a small island where she quite literally saved all their lives by digging for and discovering a fresh water spring. They managed to get to Sumatra but were rounded up by the Japanese and sent to the Padang P.O.W. camp. No rations were permitted for Judy but she overcame this by stalking and killing her own food — rats, lizards and snakes. She also struck up a remarkable partnership with another prisoner of war, a young member of the RAF named Frank Williams, which lasted till the day she died. Thin, half starved, always on the prowl, she had nevertheless recognized in this nightmare environment the master she adored and who she undoubtedly helped to sustain during the three years he worked on the Railway of Death. Finally they sailed home together to the land of her ancestors, the England she had never seen, and there Judy was awarded the Dickin Medal, the animal equivalent of the Victoria Cross.

LEO or CANCER?
(Perhaps, like our Maltese, born on the cusp).

An earlier sea dog was Bounce, a Newfoundland of Nelson's day who lived with Admiral Collingwood aboard his ship and saw action off Cadiz. 'Bounce is my only pet just now,' the Admiral wrote at that time, 'and he is indeed a good fellow. He sleeps by the side of my cot whenever I lie in one and then marches off to be out of hearing of the guns, for he is not reconciled to them yet'. Bounce was present in the Admiral's flagship, the Royal Sovereign, at Trafalgar, sharing the honours of victory and promotion to the peerage. Collingwood wrote to his wife: 'I am out of patience with Bounce. The consequential airs he gives himself since he became a right honourable dog are insufferable. He considers it beneath his dignity to play with common dogs. This is, I think, carrying the insolence of rank to the extreme; but he is a dog that does that.'

CAPRICORN or CANCER?
(The Admiral was a LIBRA).

As Pope and Collingwood would surely agree, Bounce is a splendid name for a dog. Another in my view is Mopser — providing of course that he looks like a Mopser. But what does a Mopser look like? Walter de la Mare explains in 'The Bandog':

'Has anybody seen my Mopser?

A comely dog is he,
With hair the colour of a Charles the Fifth,
And teeth like ships at sea,
His tail it curls straight upwards,
His teeth stand two abreast,
And he answers to the simple name of Mopser,
When civilly addressed.'

I have not, as yet, been the owner of a Mopser but I did once have a dashing Dalmatian, a Libra, who went by the exotic if inappropriate name of Aeneas. (His father, an otherwise sagacious and well-balanced animal, lived his whole life in the firm but mistaken belief that the correct stance for relieving his bowels was identical to the three-legged one employed for emptying his bladder. The additional effort required for the former activity usually resulted in him falling flat in a sort of undignified rear end splits not to mention an uncomfortable degree of nervous constipation. In this connection I also had a Pekingese who could only perform the same function after propping his forelegs up against a wall in the manner of a praying mantis. This was awkward when in towns since even small dogs are properly discouraged from soiling pavements and walls do not normally exist in the middle of roads.) But to return to Aeneas. When he was still little more than a puppy I used to take him (or rather he took me) for walks in Regents Park, where, once off the lead, he would rush away on mysterious errands and excitements of his own leaving me to call his name at the top of my voice. This resulted in my making the acquaintance of several sympathetic dog owners who were always full of helpful advice and also various less sympathetic sun-bathers, lovers, and assorted would be cricketers who weren't — but it never succeeded in bringing Aeneas back until he had exhausted the possibilities of whatever adventure had happened to engage his fancy. It took a few months of this before I was forced to accept that the poor dog, always the soul of obedience in the house, far from being transformed into a demon of bloody-mindedness by the heady air of the park, was in fact simply stone deaf. (At home I am sure he had learnt to lip read.) We gave him to someone who lived in a less traffic-infested area where I trust he has enjoyed a less dangerous and happy life. But whenever I think of him and his new owners, which is often, I also think of Charles Lamb, 'the frolic and the gentle', who was bequeathed, for similar reasons, a dog called Dash by the poet Thomas Hood. Hood had described him as 'truant curly, but for a spaniel wondrous surly' and he soon had the essayist under his paw. Lamb had hitherto enjoyed long solitary rambles but these had to stop because Dash 'when out would never go anywhere but where it pleased himself. In the Regents Park in particular Dash had his quasi master completely at his mercy, for the moment they got through the ring he used to squeeze himself through the railing, and disappear for half an hour together in the then enclosed and thickly planted greensward, knowing perfectly well that Lamb did not dare to move from the spot where he had disappeared, till he thought proper to show himself again. And they used to take their walk there oftener than any other, precisely because Dash liked it and Lamb did not.'

When looking for a cottage in the country (presumably to better accommodate Dash) Lamb was accosted by an indignant local resident.'Your dog has been chasing my sheep,' he exclaimed angrily. 'Chase a sheep,' the essayist replied mildly, 'he would not chase a Lamb!'

He finally transferred Dash to Coventry Patmore who recorded that 'his wild and wilful ways were a pure imposition upon the easy temper of Lamb and that as soon as he found himself in the hands of one who knew what dog decorum was, he subsided into the best bred and best behaved of his species.'

SCORPIO or VIRGO?

(Charles Lamb was an AQUARIAN. Mr Patmore on the other hand was born on July 23rd, right on the CANCER-LEO cusp, a pretty formidable combination for even the most wilful of dogs.)

Whatever their signs or their names, it will be agreed that dogs differ in many respects from people. Mark Twain made this clear in 'Pudd'nhead Wilson's Calendar':

'If you pick up a starving dog and make him prosperous, he will not bite you. That is the principal difference between a dog and a man.'

Napoleon noted another. When riding over the field of Bassano after the battle he noticed a dog still guarding the body

of his slain master. The Emperor turned to his staff and said:
'There gentlemen — that dog teaches us a lesson of humanity.'

But what do dogs think of people? Well, G.K. Chesterton
provides a possible answer in this extract from 'The Song
of Quoodle':

'They havent got no noses,
The fallen sons of Eve
Even the smell of roses
Is not what they supposes
But more than mind discloses
And more than men believe . . .

The brilliant smell of water
The brave smell of a stove
The smell of dew and thunder
The old bones buried under
Are things in which they blunder
And err, if left alone.

The wind from winter forest
The scent of scentless flowers
The breath of brides' adorning
The smell of snare and warning
The smell of Sunday morning
God gave to us for ours.

And Quoodle here discloses
All things that Quoodle can
They haven't got no noses
They haven't got no noses
And goodness only knowses
The Noselessness of Man.'

DOGS NOW

In spite of our noselessness, or more probably because of it, we continue to share our lives with dogs. We may not be able to sniff the brilliant smell of water but most of us probably wish we could and it is both reassuring and stimulating to have someone around who can. The sense of a dog complements that of a man, the mysteries of which only he is aware lighten the complexities of our own, problems which are peculiarly canine help keep human ones in proportion. Every dog owner will have their particular memory, their special story. Here are a few.

JILLY Cooper on the subject of her English Setter, Maidstone, born April 28th 1972, a TAURUS:
'He was a beautiful dog but always seemed to look a mess because he spent so much time splashing round in the black murky brook at the bottom of our common, from which he

Jilly Cooper with Maidstone's successor, Mabel

would emerge trailing goosegrass, his coat full of burrs, and looking like a tart because up to mid thigh his legs were encased in shiny black mud. He was in fact a slob. He was also a glorious delinquent. No one could train him — not that we tried very hard at the beginning, being used to more biddable dogs, and by the time he was nine months old it was too late. I could never catch him until he chose to be caught. There was no garden fence he couldn't bash his way through. During his life we spent over £1000 having ours repaired (we thought he was probably planning a book on great escapes).

Once, on Christmas Day he ran away. Tearfully we opened our presents, half of which had 'love from Maidstone' written on them. Finally someone rang up from a council estate in Roehampton to say he'd been with them all day and had enjoyed a whole Christmas dinner of turkey.

He was passionately sociable. He loved to play with other dogs, and had a totally aberrant libido, once, rather late in life, he got interested in sex. He lost his virginity when he was two, to one of the fair dogs, while the fair was in Putney. This took place beside the coconut shies, and all the stall holders were placing bets on how long he could keep going. The result of this union was twelve puppies. Once on the trail of a bitch on the common, he was quite capable of charging five miles across main roads in pursuit of her and then mounting her from the wrong end.

Some people never forget a face, he never forgot a crutch, merrily goosing everyone who came to the house, particularly middle-aged women with skirts on the knee, whom he practically lifted off the ground. He used to greet people he'd once met, after years and years of not seeing them, with total ecstasy. His memory was phenomenal.

He also sensed disapproval. If people came to the house whom he didn't like or rather who didn't like him, he would sneak into their rooms, and eat their shoes, their belts, their childrens' toys, their books. He also enjoyed drinking noisily out of the lavatory to irritate my husband who was not his greatest fan. He and I absolutely doted on one another — I suppose we were kindred spirits. Alas, I took on a mongrel who is adorable but extremely tricky. He'd had a deprived childhood and he taught Maidstone to fight. They rampaged round the common together taking on every male dog who crossed their path. One day they killed a wild cat down by the river. After that no neighbouring animal was safe, although they never touched any of our own five cats.

Maidstone then started chasing the local hospital cats, which entailed climbing four flights up the fire escape after them, and I would suddenly see his silly spotty face grinning down at me from the hospital roof. The most terrible occasion was when I suddenly heard his bass baritone bark going on and on and on, and realized to my horror that he was on the third floor roof barking at a huge female bottom with its legs strung up in the air, undergoing some unmentionable surgery in the operating theatre. Several men in green masks with scalpels were shaking their fists at him. Afterwards barking at operations became one of his favourite pastimes. In the end, in despair, when he was five I sent him to a training kennels for a month to a retired policeman who said he could sort out any dog. He failed with Maidstone. The day he came back from the kennels he broke into the fridge, and ate eight sausage rolls, a garlic sausage, half a tin of creamed rice, and a totally frozen shepherds pie. Every time I let him off his lead he ran away, returning grinning a few hours later. A week later he killed another cat, and heart-broken I had him put down that afternoon. In a way, as Eugene O'Neill once said, it was "the end of happiness but the beginning of peace." '

She also has a mongrel called Mabel or 'Mabel on the table' because she likes leaping onto them and looking down on the world. Her father is the mongrel who taught Maidstone to be a delinquent and he met her mother (another mongrel) at a cocktail party. They immediately retired to the edge of a lily pond and the result was seven puppies one of whom was Mabel, born August 27th, 1977, a VIRGO with perhaps just a touch of LEO. Ms Cooper describes her as an insatiable huntress, 'but like the goddess Diana herself, extremely chaste and virginal. She is very timid with male dogs and always keeps her tail down to ward off any passes. Her first heat was so short that the kennels assumed she was pregnant and sent her home. She hated the kennels and lost so much weight there I decided to have her spayed.

She is a picky eater and to begin with I had to feed her by hand. Even now she often takes bones or bits of fish and meat back to her downstairs basket under the kitchen table. She is also terribly possessive about her belongings, collecting bones, rubber toys and old balls into an organized pile in her basket upstairs.

Her charm is all camouflage, restraint, subtlety. But she is also incredibly loving and happiest when she's curled up beside you on the sofa. She often sits on her own tail and we think this may be because she wants to straighten out any vulgar mongrel curl.'

A typical Virgo in fact who has been lucky enough to find an understanding PISCEAN owner. Incidentally PISCES is not a particularly compatible human sign for a Taurus dog (Maidstone) whereas it is for a Virgo one (Mabel).

THE splendid **Miss Barbara Cartland** who believes that sensible eating leads to a healthy life and has written (so far) two hundred and sixty two books to prove it, has also owned and cherished several Pekingese. One of them was Ching, 'a very determined Chinese gentleman who loved me but who was enamoured, in a raffish devil-may-care way, of a big black lady labrador who lived down the road. Scoldings, beatings, pleadings, nothing would prevent him visiting her. His infatuation cost him his life.'

Ching was in fact run over on his way to an assignation with his large lady love and Miss Cartland wrote a poem in his memory:

'You were so soft, so sweet, so small,
And yet you gave your heart and all
Your love — until you died
Walking along the wrong side
of the road.

The car didn't stop and I found you there,
Your eyes were closed and your long white fur
Was covered in blood and you didn't stir
When I called.

Such a little life, so little time
To live, and yet you were part of mine.
And I never can walk in the mud and rain
Without seeing you lying dead again
In the road.'
Ching, it would appear, was probably a GEMINI.

PAM Ayres (a PISCES) happily owns a beautiful dog called Lucy Labrador (a CANCERIAN) — surely not, one feels, the model for her poem 'Puppy Problems'. Ms Ayres has suggested the following extract:

I bought myself a puppy
And I hoped in time he might
Become my friend and ward off
Things that go bump in the night,
So I put him in a shoe box
And at home I took him out,
And then began to learn
What owning puppies is about.

I bought a book on training
And I read it all one night,
And when we set off out
I really thought we'd got it right,
With titbits in my coat

To give him once he got the knack,
But he didn't so I couldn't
So *I* ate them coming back.

When I commanded "Heel!"
He never seemed to take the point
But galloped on half-strangled,
Tugging my arm out of joint.
He jumped up people's clothes,
The cleaning bills I had to pay!
And when I shouted 'Here!'
He turned and ran the other way.

This one's birth sign defies definition. Perhaps it's safer just to say he's a typical 'Ayrean' and leave it at that!

SOME years ago the writer, **Willis Hall**, was recuperating in a remote country cottage after a serious operation. The success of his convalescence depended in large part on two factors — sleeping pills to ensure a good night's rest and a Dalmatian to act as watchdog. For most of the time each satisfactorily fulfilled their different functions but at certain irregular periods and for no particular reason the dog would start to bark at three a.m. and continued doing so with hardly a break until dawn, sitting up very straight in his basket looking more like an alert human sentry than a canine one. On the first of these occasions Willis, having satisfied himself that there were no nocturnal intruders in the vicinity, did his best to calm the dog, begging him to be quiet so that he could resume his slumbers. The dog continued to bark. There was only one solution. Willis sandwiched one of his precious sleeping pills between two pieces of bread, the dog ate it and peace was restored. This operation was repeated whenever necessary. The Dalmatian suffered no ill effects, Willis Hall made a complete recovery and only his doctor was left rather puzzled by his apparently increasing reliance on sleeping pills. (Mr Hall was not certain as to the Dalmatian's birth sign. Would you care to hazard a guess?)

MISS Elspeth March has another claim to fame besides being a beautiful and talented actress. She is the owner of a rather special Shih Tzu called Tukka (and is contemplating acquiring another to be called Bib in order to complete the double). In 1976 Miss March appeared with Miss Maggie Smith in a play at the Vaudeville Theatre entitled 'Snap'. Her part was that of a breeder of Shih Tzus and the script called for a Shih Tzu to appear on stage whenever she did. After some argument Miss March was prevailed upon to draft Tukka. Although he had no previous training he proved himself a natural actor, a real pro, never missing an entrance, never looking at the audience, never bumping into the furniture and always picking up his cues. His only slight departure from the director's requirements was a tendency to exhibit proof of his *maleness* to the stalls whenever possible which slightly confused the plot since his role was that of a bitch named Bernadette. Apart from this single lapse his theatrical manners were impeccable. He always got in early to allow time for his grooming which took considerably longer than his mistress's make-up, barked in the dressing rooms but *never* in the wings and took his female co-stars, Miss Smith and Miss March, out to lunch on expenses on matinee days. Now that he is temporarily out of work he still refuses to get up before midday and when visiting the theatre cannot understand why he isn't allowed to go on stage and show them what it's all about. He is, says Elspeth, an independent character, autocratic as a cat (or a leading actor) and when he considers it time for going to bed will bark until she is forced to turn off the telly and do likewise. And he never passes the Vaudeville without looking up at the display case which was once graced by a very large photograph of himself adorned with a bright yellow sticker bearing the proud legend 'This brilliant dog — Sheridan Morley — The Tatler.'

Tukka, need one add, is a CAPRICORN.

PETER Smalley is a LIBRAN who was once a highly successful advertising executive in Australia and has now switched to the possibly less lucrative but for him more emotionally rewarding business of writing books and films in

England. He lives in the depths of the country and owns a LIBRA dog who had the disconcerting and irritating habit of rushing out of the house at dusk and disappearing into the nearest British equivalent of the antipodean bush where he remained until breakfast time the following day. After wasting the first half of many nights (which he had set aside for writing) in a fruitless search for his wandering dog Mr Smalley hit on a better and less tiring idea. Being a man of imagination he simply went and sat down on a fallen tree or a patch of grass at the edge of his local wood, closed his eyes and concentrated on exactly *how* the errant animal would visualize him at that precise moment. This telepathic process never failed. On every occasion the dog emerged from amongst the trees within minutes and obediently accompanied his master back to his house and typewriter. LIBRANS *do* need to communicate — but not always by the most orthodox methods.

OTAL communication exists between **Ms Tanya Bruce Lockhart** (a backstage luminary of such television programmes as *Aquarius*) and her dog Rikki (once described by Sir Peter Hall as an automated coffee table). They met thirteen years ago on the beach at Marbella when both were at a crisis point in their lives. Tanya was facing the problem of whether to get married and Rikki, deserted by persons unknown and on the edge of starvation, that of how to remain alive. Each immediately recognized an instinctive need for the other and since Rikki was in no condition to make the first move — one broken leg and no hair on his unbeautiful Alsatian-like mongrel head — Tanya, a typical LEO, made it for him. She fed him, set his leg, took a room for him at the exclusive Marbella Club and after many tussles with bureaucracy got him flown back to England in a tin box. On his release from quarantine he travelled by couchette to Edinburgh to join her at a rather grand grouse shooting weekend. In spite of all protests she insisted that he attend the actual shoot during which he saw a mountain hare and gave chase. The other normally disciplined dogs followed, the shoot broke up in confusion and Rikki was forthwith banned from taking part in any further such sporting occasions. This

means that Tanya doesn't participate in them either for the good
and simple reason that she won't go anywhere without him and
that includes everything from social engagements to work. That's
why, for instance, Rikki watched the television production of
Kenneth MacMillan's ballet 'Mayerling' from the Royal Box at
Covent Garden. No other accommodation was available and
everyone knew that if he wasn't there the Assistant Producer
wouldn't be there either. In the event he ate too many smoked
salmon sandwiches and drowsed off in regal splendour during
the more dramatic scenes. She takes him to Gucci or Aspreys to
choose his evening collars and on one such occasion a surprised
American lady exclaimed loudly (and not *entirely* untruthfully)

'What a hideous dog!' 'You don't look so hot yourself,' Ms Lockhart said sweetly, 'but I'm sure you have a beautiful nature too.' It was, she explains, an instinctive reaction, like springing to the defence of one's own child. She admits that sometimes it may all seem to go a bit too far, particularly when her own mother starts sending her cards on Mothers Day. But the point, she says, is that she and Rikki each fulfils an essential need for the other and that's about as satisfactory an emotional relationship as anyone has the right to hope for. She has never for one second regretted the decision made thirteen years ago and nor, obviously, has Rikki. She is still unmarried and he is still alive, an estimated fifteen years old now, a bit arthritic in the hips, a Mitty-Alsatian who defers modestly to real ones, a meticulous cleaner of his only white leg and paw, a total ignorer of bitches on heat. 'He hasn't got any balls,' Ms Lockhart says cheerfully, 'never had.' Rikki grins patiently and with immense charm. He has heard her tell all these stories before and he isn't going to spoil a good one now. The understanding between them is absolute. They are a double act, never boring, never bored. More than an act, they are a reality to be envied. She doesn't know his birth sign but on reflection thinks it may be VIRGO. Rikki nods, confirming her opinion. LEO and VIRGO are not ordinarily considered as the most compatible of signs — but then Rikki and Ms Lockhart are not subject to ordinary rules. She told me that when he dies she will never even try to replace him because it would be impossible, and this reminded me of something else written by Walter Scott: 'The misery of keeping a dog is his dying so soon. But, to be sure, if he lived for fifty years and then died, what would become of me?' It's an observation which, I think you'll agree, is well worth pondering.

¶T is good to know that Scott's love of dogs is remembered by another great artist of our own day. **Sir Alec Guinness's** description of his dog (an ARIES incidentally):

'Walter Abbotsford, of that ilk, was named after Sir Walter Scott, who was devoted to Dandy Dinmonts. Born 2nd April 1974. Run over by a milk float January 1978; pelvis crushed, leg broken and stomach split open. Still very much alive, with a surprising turn of speed and totally delighted with life. July 1979 killed a polecat. Looks on himself as a mighty hunter and is an accomplished underground tunneller. These days he comes indoors when he sees the milkman arrive and tries to kill him through the window. One day may succeed. Obsessional about cheese and squirrels. Good at worrying Income Tax demands.'

S PEAKING of famous men, there are some who one instinctively feels, *must* own dogs, who one cannot help *associating* with dogs, who, let's face it, have at times even managed to *look* like dogs. How wrong one can be.

From: CLEMENT FREUD, M.P.   3380

HOUSE OF COMMONS
LONDON SWIA OAA
01-219 3408

21st May, 1979

R. Houghton Esq.,
Editorial Director,
Elm Tree Books Ltd.,
Garden House,
57-59 Long Acre,
London WC2E 9JZ.

Dear Mr. Houghton,

I do not have a dog;
I once had a ferret.

Yours sincerely,

Clement Freud MP

But let's assume that *you* want one — or a second, or a third. What about the all important question of Sex?

Bitch's Lib?

'If possible get a bitch, even though her twice yearly season occasions a certain amount of inconvenience . . . . a bitch is more faithful than a dog, the intricacies of her mind are finer, richer and more complex than his, and her intelligence is generally greater. I have known very many dogs and can say with firm conviction that of all creatures, the one nearest to man in the fineness of its perceptions and in its capacity to render true friendship, is a bitch. Strange that in English her name has become a term of abuse.'

Konrad Lorenz in *Man Meets Dog*

Male Chauvinism?

'When it comes to sex — and doesn't it always? — it's a matter of personal preference. Some people say that bitches are more affectionate than dogs, although I have not personally found this to be true. Dogs are certainly less trouble. They do not have to go through the ordeal of being on heat, an awkward time that comes twice a year and lasts three weeks on each occasion. Unless you want to breed, I would advise a dog.'

Buster Lloyd-Jones in *Come Into My World*

It must be of some comfort to anyone who has ever been racked with delicious indecision when faced with a swarm of delectable puppies to know that even the greatest experts are not always in agreement about such a fundamental point as sex. But perhaps Mr Lloyd-Jones should have the last word:

'I know with absolute certainty that it is the puppy who will choose *you*.'

But, *you* can choose his Birth Sign!

DOGS FOR ALL TIME

You can meet and study many of the most famous dogs in the world at any time you wish. Here are just four of them. The first two are in Venice, the third in Madrid and the fourth in London. Their combined ages amount to over fifteen hundred years. Number one is the little dog in the bottom left hand corner of Carpaccio's painting 'The Vision Of St Augustine' and in his beautiful book *Animals and Men* Kenneth Clark says of him: 'A fluffy dog has even been allowed into St Augustine's study, where he sits most unexpectedly, among the armillary spheres and astrolabes . . . (and) seems to be receiving the vision of St Jerome's death before it was vouchsafed to St Augustine'. Number two is by the same artist in his painting 'Two Courtesans': 'One could perhaps deduce from Carpaccio's whole approach to life that he loved dogs, and he has left us one of the most completely realized dogs in painting, who sits at the feet of a seated courtesan in the picture in the Correr (museum) that Ruskin praised so extravagantly'. Next time you're in Venice take a close look at these two immortals, or, if you can't manage to get there, buy postcard prints of the originals. The fluffy dog who's bright button eye so clearly sees the future must surely be a Piscean or a Cancerian. And the other one, allowing his front paws to rest listlessly in the listless hand of the courtesan at whose feet he sits, his face turned towards us, its expression inscrutable, yet reflecting the scenes he must have witnessed, the frailties and the toughness of human behaviour — a Scorpio perhaps, an Arien who's seen it all? Number three has got to be a Capricorn. He is a dog painted by Velasquez; 'the saturnine animal that sits in front of the dwarfs in 'Las Meninas' is not only the greatest dog in art but a somewhat disturbing commentary on the gentle, courtly scene depicted. He seems to echo the contempt of the disdainful dwarf behind him . . . whoever is meant to be impressed by these royal personages, we are not'.

Lastly, Hogarth's beloved pug, Trump, in his famous self portrait. 'Hogarth took this solid, four-square, down-to-earth pug as his emblem, and gives it a degree of reality — outside the frame, in the 'real' world — which he denies to his own portrait. "It had been jocularly observed by him," wrote Samuel Ireland, "that there was a close resemblance between his own countenance and that of his favourite dog, who was his faithful friend and companion for many years" '. William Hogarth was a true Scorpio. And Trump? A Taurus? A Leo? They're at the Tate. Why not go and see what you think?

In the same book Lord Clark quotes what must be not only one of the most ancient but also one of the most moving passages ever to be written about any dog. It is taken from Homer's Odyssey and tells of the moment when Odysseus, disguised from Penelope and her suitors, is recognized by his old dog. 'There, full of vermin, lay Argus, the hound. But directly he became aware of Odysseus' presence he wagged his tail and dropped his ears, though he lacked the strength now to come any nearer to his master. Yet Odysseus saw him out of the corner of his eye, and brushed a tear away . . .'

Homer goes on to say that no sooner had Argus set eyes on his master after those nineteen years, that he succumbed to the black hand of death.

Truly a dog for all time, and, whatever may have been his birth sign, I can only wish you, under different circumstances of course, another like him.

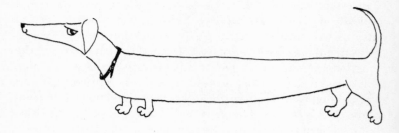

A LAST WORD

If you own a dog and would like to send us any funny, poignant or unusual stories about him/her the author or publishers would welcome them for use in a possible sequel.

If, on the other hand, you really prefer cats, do please send us some stories about them. But hurry, we're working on Astrology for Cats right now.